YOU ARE YOUR INSTRUMENT

The Definitive Musician's Guide To Practice and Performance

BY JULIE LYONN LIEBERMAN

Foreword by: W. Donald Cooke M.D.
Illustrations by Reuben Butchart

Second Edition
Huiksi Music, New York, NY

YOU ARE YOUR INSTRUMENT:
The Definitive Musician's Guide To Practice and Performance

By Julie Lyonn Lieberman

Published by:
Huiksi Music
Post Office Box 495
New York, NY 10024-3202 U.S.A.

Graphic Design: Loren Moss
Illustrations: Reuben Butchart
Cover Photo: Will Ryan
Glossary Photos: Randall Wallace
Editor: Nan Gatewood
Medical definitions by W. Donald Cooke, M.D.
Photo model: Michael Schwartz, Physical Fitness Consultant

Disclaimer:
This book does not attempt to replace medical attention as needed.
When injured, it is important to check into the problem with the
appropriate medical authority to determine proper action.

Library of Congress Cataloging in Publication Data
Lieberman, Julie Lyonn
You Are Your Instrument:
The Definitive Musician's Guide to Practice and Performance

by Julie Lyonn Lieberman
Bibliography
Includes index.
1. Music   2. Musicians   3. Music Instruction   4. Music Study
5. Musicians - Anatomy   6. Musicians - Muscular Injury
1. Title
MT2.L716Y6 1991   780.7   91-71458
ISBN 1-879730-20-0 $20.00 Softcover

 2 3 4 5 6 7 8 9 10 Printing 91

Dedication

This book is dedicated to William Henry, who always encouraged my individuality as a musician, and whose last concerts were played connected to an intravenous feeder. He died too young but not without filling the world with beautiful music.

Become quite still until you no longer think, want,
feel anything.
Sense your soul a little above your chest.
Let its radiance slowly permeate your whole body
both upwards and downwards at the same time.
Open your head on top in the center, a little towards the back
and let the current that hovers above you there
like a dense sphere, enter into you.
Let the current slowly fill you from head to foot
and continue flowing.

KARLHEINZ STOCKHAUSEN, ARRIVAL

Acknowledgments

I give thanks to my private students and the students I've worked with at New York University, Manhattan School of Music, Berklee College of Music, and the New England Conservatory. They have given me the opportunity, through their enthusiasm, dedication and trust, to experiment with, explore, and fine-tune the material in this book on the deepest, most gratifying levels.

I would also like to thank my teachers of the body and mind: Judah Kataloni (Alexander Technique); Moshe Feldenkrais; Michael Reed Gach (Acupressure and Acuyoga); Martin Ravitsky (Shiatsu); Ananda Ashram's yearly Healing Arts Festival; Dr. Charles Ridley for his preventive chiropractics; Therese Bertherat for her book "The Body Has Its Reasons"; Milton Ward's "The Brilliant Function of Pain"; my dance and yoga teachers; Ray Evans Harrell who taught me how to create sound from my whole, integrated self; Ken Guilmartin for leading me in numerous explorations of the place where words, sounds, movement, and individuality meet in the creation of art; Robert Fritz for his genius for structure and for teaching me the power of vision and truth; and Kalen Hammann for guiding me in the formulation of a new foundation and the development of my leadership abilities.

Special thanks to my parents for teaching me the power of creative thought and for encouraging me to give form to my ideas; and to Swansea Blue Benham and Mark Kindschi for encouraging me to finally finish this book.

My deepest thanks go to the people without whom this book would not have been possible: graphic designer Loren Moss, editor Nan Gatewood, photographers Will Ryan and Randall Wallace, illustrator Reuben Butchart, Jane and Happy Traum of Homespun Tapes for making this book into a video, and to John Glasel, Danstan R. Hutchinson, Don Cooke, Tim and Vicki Richards, and Bill Ochs for their generous support and advice.

Foreword

The athletic feats required of the musician can often lead to injury. On occasion, these problems can be severe enough to cause significant artistic and financial difficulties. The pianist with the painful hand may, quite appropriately, seek the advice of a physician regarding this dilemma. Unfortunately, unless she is very lucky, the advice she gets is likely to be a curt dismissal to go home and rest. The doctor, you see, may be a hand specialist who just returned from the operating room after reattaching some poor fellow's severed hand. The fact is, most physicians are not familiar with the field of music medicine, and the complaints that may spell disaster for a professional musician are often not viewed as disastrous by the doctor. Fortunately, this is beginning to change.

Recently, the field of music medicine has blossomed. There are clinics now dedicated exclusively to the care of performing artists. A journal, "Medical Problems of Performing Artists" has recently been published which is entirely devoted to this problem. Some mainstream medical periodicals, such as the "Cleveland Clinic Quarterly" and "Seminars in Neurology," have published whole issues on the medical problems of performing artists. Despite this attention, there still exists a wide chasm between the training of physicians and musicians, which can make dialog awkward. Doctors, trained as they are in the scientific method, tend to view the body largely as a machine composed of interrelated organ systems, which occasionally require repair, usually after they have broken down. Musicians, on the other hand, often perceive the body in a more integrated and intuitive way.

During the many years that I have been immersed in both disciplines — as a fiddler and as an internist — it has become clear to me that a bridge between this philosophical and perceptual gap may benefit us both. Doctors need to understand the psyche of the musician, and learn to emphasize prevention. Musicians need to understand how the various parts of the body function together, and how to take advantage of the wonderful interplay of muscle, bone, and nerve which ultimately act in concert to produce music. Between the scientific and the intuitive views there is plenty of common ground; we only need explore it. This book makes an important step in that direction.

Drawing on years of teaching experience, Julie Lyonn Lieberman functions as our guide. She places strong emphasis on avoiding physical tension and creating the correct balance within the body as a whole. The chapters are designed for the musician of any level to come to an appreciation of what exactly is required for playing an instrument, how this can go awry, how to correct it, or who to see if you can't. The scope is comprehensive, and includes information from many different conventional and alternative disciplines. The goal here is more skillful, and healthier musicians. In the pursuit of this aim, we all have something to learn.

W. Donald Cooke M.D.
Horseheads, New York
April, 1991

$\mathcal{T}$ABLE OF CONTENTS

YOU ARE YOUR INSTRUMENT

Listening With the Musician's Ear

The current statistics regarding muscle-related problems for musicians are alarmingly high. The New England Journal of Medicine cites that 50% of all professional musicians suffer from varying levels of muscular injury while other studies claim that the figures are as high as 75%! While amateur musicians may not spend as much time on the instrument as professionals, they are more likely to play incorrectly, thus exposing themselves to injury just as readily.

Historically, international reports of overuse syndrome among musicians can be found in medical literature dating as far back as 1830 in as many as 21 books and 54 articles. Even then, the disorder was said to result from the overuse of the affected parts. While there were several theories regarding the etiology — namely that a lesion existed either in the central nervous system or that the condition was a primary muscle disorder — it was agreed upon that total rest from the mechanical use of the hand (or affected body part) was the only effective treatment.

The number of names for the condition included occupational cramp, musician's cramp, occupational neurosis, professional impotence, craft palsy, occupational overstrain, fatigue disease, over-fatigue, overuse, and exhaustion neurosis. Musicians were second only to writers and, according to Hunter J.H. Fry in his article "Overuse Syndrome in Musicians — 100 Years Ago," (*The Medical Journal of Australia*, December 1986) two key insights were discussed in the late 1800's: that the condition was caused by repetitive muscular movement beyond the natural capacity of the individual and that constant and even forcible intermittent muscular use was not nearly as injurious as prolonged contraction.

These are key points to consider because they illustrate the importance of conscious attention to muscle use while playing, the need for rest periods within the practice session, and the fact that every one of us is built differently and that we must be aware of our own physical and mental capacities.

Considering the musical and financial pressures today's musicians weather in order to create music, growing problems with tension and injury are not surprising. These pressures have increased parallel to the demands of a note-perfect-hungry technology, the media's infatuation with prodigies and celebrity musicians, the competition for jobs and status limited to a privileged few, and a country that, over the past decades, has decreased levels of government support, and has relegated the arts to a position of relative unimportance in the education system.

Our music education system has traditionally favored technique, mechanically correct physical movement, ear-training, theory, and repertoire. Until recently, there has been an indifference in conservatory training to balancing those subjects with what I call "taking care of business": training musicians to create their professional lives intelligently rather than haphazardly, as well as providing them with a working knowledge of how to use their bodies correctly so that they may have long and healthy careers. Private instruction, of course, tends to mirror this imbalance, with few exceptions.

While business matters aren't the primary focus of this book, they must be mentioned because the psychological stress that comes from living hand to mouth and "groping in the dark" professionally can be a major contributing factor to muscular stress. The largest contributing factor, though, is overuse of the muscles in repetitive activity; i.e. practicing for too many hours a day is detrimental to the body's health! The cumulative effect on the tissues can eventually exceed the body's physiological limit and injury can impede or end a career.

Take a moment and ask yourself this question: "Do I play no matter what my body feels like with the idea that I'll deal with injury later if and when it comes up?" If the answer is yes, then you are a member of the Injury-Prone Club. In my fifteen years of work with musicians with muscular problems such as chronic tension, tendinitis, and lower back pain, that mind-set has been present in every single one of them. As a matter of fact, the more pervasive the mind-set, the more serious the injury.

Keep in mind that if you use your body consciously, you will increase your quality of experience, health and longevity, and you will sound better. Tension reduces muscular suppleness and fluidity; tone goes downhill as does the availability of effortless speed.

Knowledge of the muscular structure and its upkeep is a vital part of dance and athletic training. Musicians use their bodies in just as demanding and rigorous a fashion to produce music, yet our education focuses almost exclusively on visual and motor skills. Even aural skills receive less attention than visual and motor ones. Body knowledge is often limited to the hands, yet it's still surprising to learn how few musicians actually know where their fingers muscles are! We have become excellent at tuning in to one small aspect of music-making to the exclusion of the rest of our body, our breath, and our very heart and soul.

In 1972 I began to experience pressure in my ears. The ear doctor told me that there was nothing wrong. I started Sarah Lawrence College that fall. My new college-appointed violin teacher was a major classical player on the New York City scene. He'd just completed a series of cortisone injections for chronic muscular spasms and after several months of not being able to

play at all, had started studying the Alexander Technique — a gentle form of physical therapy that teaches body alignment and retrains the muscles to function with a minimum amount of tension and effort.

Upon his recommendation I began Alexander lessons. To my surprise, my "hearing problem" disappeared within a month. It had been caused by extreme muscular tension in my neck from playing the violin. Of course, it had never occurred to the ear doctor to ask questions about my major area of interest.

This experience started me on an exploration of alternative approaches to healing and to music-making. In my personal odyssey as a student of the healing arts and as a performer of classical, folk, jazz and New Age music, I've met many injured musicians who either consider their pain as a normal state of affairs or have received inadequate or even damaging medical attention.

When I first began work on this book in 1976, I received a mixed response. I was politely told by several famous classical players that the only way to become a great musician was to practice and ignore all possible diversions, including physical pain. Publishers told me that the book was a wonderful idea but they had no idea how to market it. I did receive tremendous encouragement from a number of music educators, including my first violin teacher, the late Samuel Applebaum, as well as from musicians who had damaged their bodies from practice and performance.

The term Music Medicine was coined in 1982 shortly after pianist Gary Graffman brought the unique health problems of the musician to the public's attention. A successful concert pianist, Graffman developed a problem using the fourth and fifth fingers of his right hand after many years of prolonged practice each day. It is believed that his injury stemmed from using his third finger to play octaves rather than his fourth or fifth finger. But it took eighteen doctors with eighteen different diagnoses before he found a doctor who finally acknowledged that his injury might have been caused by playing the piano!

It's interesting to note that until his problem appeared, Graffman had never given the slightest thought as to how he played the piano. Another important factor intrinsic to his injury was the number of years he ignored warning signals; he basically waited until he couldn't function properly before he sought help. Many musicians hope that their problems will magically disappear if ignored; others are afraid to acknowledge injury lest word leak out and dry up future work.

Thanks to Graffman's media crusade as well as subsequent symposia and articles on the subject, the field of Music Medicine developed out of the recognition that musicians sustain physical injuries unique to their craft, requiring doctors who understand the physical challenge of practice and performance and as such, know how to give proper diagnosis and treatment.

Many doctors and clinics now devote their time exclusively to injured musicians or performing artists. This doesn't necessarily mean, however, that they have all the answers. It's still essential for you to understand how your body works, how injury is created, and what your options are, once injured.

This mounting interest in the musician's well-being signifies a readiness on our part to develop our music-making from a new perspective. "No pain, no gain" is no longer the motto of the musical athlete because a lifetime commitment to music now includes choosing quality of experience, an active role in taking responsibility for health, and a recognition of the ramifications of this shift.

We are on the edge of making a quantum leap, of creating a vital new contribution to music that is transformational for the audience as well as the performer.

Our body-mind has an internal intelligence that we must learn to trust. Pain is a valuable signal telling us, if we listen carefully enough with our finely trained musician's ears, how and where we are abusing ourselves. To make beautiful music, we need our body's full participation: pain-free, graceful, and fluidly alive.

The less attention we pay to how we use our bodies, the greater the damage we incur and the more we actually disassociate from our individuality and life spirit. Ease and joy in the creation of music is available to us now if we desire it. The shift need only begin with choice and commitment.

> *Whatever you can do or dream you can do, begin it.*
>
> *Boldness has genius, power, and magic in it.*
>
> GOETHE

YOUR MIND

The Power of the Mind

PHYSIOLOGICAL CHANGES THROUGH CONCEPTUALIZATION

I was performing at a healing arts festival in 1979 the first time I truly considered the magnificent power of the mind. There was a ninety-six year-old yogi visiting from India; he'd been practicing yoga daily since age five. He demonstrated his ability to quicken and slow his heartbeat, control pain, and place his body in seemingly impossible positions. He even showed us how breathing could be approached as a fine art with numerous and precise variations.

While I was extremely impressed with his deep power of concentration, it was a private talk with him later that I will never forget.

He told me that he'd grown tired of having white hair — it had turned white when he was in his fifties — and that he was changing it back to its original color. I thought he meant that he was about to have it dyed. He called me over to look at his scalp. I'll never forget the wave of goose bumps that swept through me when I walked over to take a look. There was one inch of newly grown black hair throughout his scalp!

You may think this impossible; all I can tell you is that I saw it with my own eyes.

The capabilities the yogi demonstrated had been cultivated through carefully guided mental development. There are numerous examples of sophisticated mind-to-body connections in the world: people who walk on burning hot coals without injury, break wood with the side of the hand, fast for days, accurately "see" into an individual's history and future, or perform tremendous athletic feats, to name a few. All of this is, in one way or another, connected to the power of the mind.

There are many musicians who've told me that when they merely think of an upcoming performance, their heart rate increases and they start to sweat. Most musicians assume that this type of physical response is beyond their control. It isn't. The very fact that there are specific physical manifestations in response to specific thoughts, proves the mind-to-body connection. But, because we have not been encouraged or taught how to develop this particular type of interaction, few of us even know how to create an effective interplay between the mind and body.

Unfortunately, music education has placed most of its emphasis on the development of physical skills through following written notation and mindless repetition.

As musicians we, too, are engaged in mind-to-body development. In addition, our music-making calls upon our aural, tactile, and kinesthetic awareness. Conscious mental direction through conceptualization and imaging can effect enormous impact on how our bodies perform as well as the degree of mental and physical effort we expend.

I would like to encourage you to use this book as a stepping stone into the development of a new orientation: use it to evolve new definitions, attitudes, and practice habits. You will find that the cultivation of these new mental skills will facilitate a shift to greater awareness, fluidity, pleasure, and creative individuality in practice and performance. The outcome will be felt in your body, heard in your music, and experienced by your audience.

My Name is Effort

Most people, when they make a commitment to learning an instrument or becoming a professional musician, begin to practice diligently, hour after hour. They focus on getting through the music, and doing it right. I know I did! Eventually my hands and arms would tire, shoulders throb in pain, and shoulder blades ache. If I felt that I hadn't made enough progress I would continue practicing until my lower back also sang the song of Effort. Perhaps a few more passages had been learned, a few rough sections ironed out, a bit more memorized.

I had also, however, mentally mapped the piece out with "color-coded" areas: "red" for the passages to fear and tighten up on because of the degree of difficulty (often even unconsciously speeding up in these sections), and "blue" for the easy ones. I certainly hadn't been breathing beyond the minimum to survive. The practice session generally ended when I was mentally or physically exhausted or numb, and functioning automatically.

After a few days like this, I would guiltily take a day or two off from practicing. Perhaps not intentionally, perhaps the day(s) just slipped by. Or maybe I would wake up in the morning with a stiff neck or nagging back pain and decide to rest. The thought of practice seemed synonymous with exertion and I usually had to struggle against a mounting resistance in order to get myself to practice.

After a day or two of rest, the alarm light would go on with any number of messages: "You won't know the material for your lesson and you'll make a fool of yourself," or "You have a concert coming up — get back to work," or even "You'll never be a great musician if you take time off." Sometimes it was a nonverbal message like general anxiety, a knot in the stomach, or an overwhelming feeling of missing playing or missing music.

If this sounds familiar, then your name may be Effort and you too have probably been duped by the educational system into believing that suffering equals progress, that you must manipulate yourself into action, that breath is not an integral part of the life of the music, or that there's only one correct way to hold your instrument. These beliefs are the seeds of potential injury and engender deficits in the vibrancy of life and music.

With so much emphasis on technique, correctly placed sounds, and impressing one's listeners with perfection, most musicians have neglected to develop their quality of experience while playing. Many musicians' expectations are generally so low in this area that they consider themselves fortunate when they play well, when they don't suffer "too much," or when they don't make "too many" mistakes.

Tragically, musicians have given away their instinctive knowledge of their bodies, no longer able to trust what their body tells them, particularly if it cries out in warning or contradicts instructions from "an expert" or authority.

Those of you who have no intention of performing may be shaking your heads and saying "My name couldn't possibly be Effort," but unless you have chosen a quality experience in each moment, that old Puritan work ethic creeps in like a virus saying "Suffer now on earth for the benefits in Heaven." The "should's," the right way even if it feels wrong,* the tendency toward a mindless routine, are all paths that potentially lead to physical injury and lifelessness.

Quality of Experience

There is little reason to develop your playing ability in order to sound good or transform and inspire others if you are suffering physically or forcing yourself to practice. Consider placing equal importance on what you want to feel like when you play and what kind of experience you want to have. Imagine enjoying playing so much that you look forward to it every day!

A quality ten minutes during which you are focused and balanced and playing from your whole, involved self (body, spirit, and mind) can produce better results than five compulsive hours of mindless repetition enforced with guilt or will-power manipulation. Passages can be practiced in your mind while doing other activities (see *Visualization and the Imagistic Mind*) to give specific direction to the sound and physical experience you want to create while playing.

*U*nfortunately, by the nineteenth century, art and artful skill (techne) yielded to technique, and, more recently, to technology. And skills that were once grounded in the insight that comes from the rhythm of awakening pulsing through the total body-mind-being became the mechanical artifacts of a humanity increasingly fragmented and cut off from its own depths in psyche.

JEAN HOUSTON, THE POSSIBLE HUMAN

---

*When a student says that something feels wrong even though it looks as if he or she is doing it correctly, it is probably because the student has mastered the outer shell of the shape or action, but is using his or her muscles incorrectly and doesn't in fact "have it" yet. Teachers who encourage their students to continue performing an action that hurts and feels uncomfortable may in fact be encouraging the student to ignore important physical signals.

THE CONDITIONAL PRACTICE SESSION

Much of the effort and lack of quality of experience involved in music-making can be attributed to the strong beliefs and assumptions we make about exactly what must happen during our practice time in order to "make progress" or in order to become a "great musician."

These beliefs include judgments about the amount of time and repetition necessary, the ideal physical environment, the ideal emotional or psychological state, the amount of material that must be covered, the assumption that the instrument must be present in order to practice, as well as a pervasive attitude that practice isn't the "real thing," that it's just an intermediate step toward something that is always in the future.

Unfortunately, most of these beliefs are seldom questioned and are often held as truth or fact. For instance, if you believe that your instrument must be present in order for you to be able to practice and make progress (which, by the way, is not true) then progress will be halted or reversed if your instrument is in the repair shop, you are sick in bed, on vacation, riding a bus, or cleaning your home! Momentum is stopped or dissipated, negative feelings run rampant, and you must then find a way to rev up your energy to get started again once your instrument is back in hand. (See *Visualization and the Imagistic Mind*.)

Beliefs are powerful because most of our actions, mental and physical, are based on them. They enable or disable. They catalyze or limit and damage. A priority system based on false or limiting beliefs can easily lead to physical stress and abuse, especially when concerns about "hard results" creep in.

In addition, beliefs and expectations regarding what is necessary to create the "perfect practice session" often get transferred to the "perfect performance" or the "perfect performance conditions."

Musical Development

Consider your evolution as an artist from another standpoint. Imagine that your music does not spring solely from your fingers; imagine that it comes from all of who you are — from your psyche as well as your physiology.

Therefore, everything you do each day that improves your:

- mind-to-body connection (typing, exercise, sports, yoga, meditation, etc.);

- ability to acknowledge and articulate your emotions as well as your uniquely individual life perspective;

- ability to listen with great focus;

- ability to identify muscular or mental/physical dysfunction and make a perceptual and functional shift in order to address it (through bodywork and various forms of therapy);

can be tapped to improve your playing ability.

In addition, time spent practicing through mental imaging can be just as productive — if not more productive — than actual time on the instrument.

Two sticks lie on the ground. Only a cognitive leap can prompt a person to rub them together to make fire. Similarly, you must make the connective leap to use all of the mental and physical resources you've developed in various areas of your life, applying them to the act of making music.

We may observe how natural practices have given way to acquired methods, to "professional" methods, and that society in general refuses to allow the individual the right to employ the natural method, forcing him instead to learn the accepted way before it will permit him to work.

MOSHE FELDENKRAIS, AWARENESS THROUGH MOVEMENT

Take a look at the beliefs and expectations you have about "should's" and "should nots" regarding what it takes to make progress.

Imagine having a relationship with a person exactly equivalent to your current relationship to your instrument! Try keeping a diary for a few days describing your thoughts and feelings during your practice time, then rewrite the entries translating your relationship with your instrument into a relationship with a real person!

EXAMPLE:

Diary Entry of Practice Session

Monday: I knew that I'd regressed so I practiced twice as much today to make up for yesterday's "vacation." I had to force myself the first hour and then I gradually got going. My back felt stiff, and my shoulders burned by the end of two hours but I kept playing to get in that third hour. I also noticed that I ignored paying attention to my posture, and whether or not I was breathing, saying to myself "...later, once I finish learning this piece." I thought about a lot of other things while I was mastering the passages with which I have been having difficulty. When I finally played through the whole piece at the end of my practice session, I didn't really enjoy the music because I was too busy trying to do everything correctly. The next day, I woke up with a stiff neck and felt totally out of sorts.

Translation Into A Relationship with a Real Person

Monday: I knew that I'd have to work harder when I saw John today because I didn't see him yesterday, so I scheduled a longer visit. We ate his favorite food and went to a few art openings because he likes to do that and I felt I had to make up to him. My feet and back hurt from dragging around town so much but I ignored the pain. I also ignored him, and thought about a lot of other things when he was talking to me. When we made love that night I didn't really have a good time because I was busy trying to do everything correctly. By the time we went to sleep, I had a stiff neck and was feeling totally out of sorts.

The Brain

THE LEFT AND RIGHT HEMISPHERES

Knowing about your brain may not strike you as helpful to your musicianship, yet it's been found that an understanding of basic mental functions can facilitate enormous changes in practice and performance.

Our brain contains two hemispheres: left and right. Each hemisphere controls physical movement on the opposite side of the body and governs certain thought processes. To establish a clear understanding of how the brain functions, we'll discuss the two hemispheres as if they had totally different functions. In reality there are varying amounts of cross-over function depending on factors including hand dominance, education, and cultural background.

The brain is an immensely complex subject, with new discoveries constantly outdating old theories. For our purposes here, it's important to be aware of the fact that there is a relationship between the cortex (the two hemispheres) and the two nervous systems. In fact, I've found that musicians benefit from imagining the sympathetic nervous system as left-brain activated and the parasympathetic as right-brain activated. Whether or not this is scientifically correct, the approach works, and I will refer to these relationships elsewhere in this book as if they were fact. You will find that it is much easier to relax (via access to the parasympathetic nervous system) if you use imagery (a right-brain function), than if you verbally instruct yourself (a left-brain function) to "relax" or "calm down."

Left-Hemisphere Education

We live in an increasingly verbal world in which our educational system stresses the development of verbal skills to better prepare us for success.

LEFT HEMISPHERE

Rational
Verbal
Analytical
Sequential
Linear

RIGHT HEMISPHERE

Creative
Intuitive
Imagistic (pictures, maps, faces)
Spatial
Wholistic
Synthesizing
Musical

There are also two branches of the autonomic nervous system:

THE SYMPATHETIC NERVOUS SYSTEM

- fight/fright/flight
- governs total body moves through activation of the larger muscle groups
- activates and heightens heartbeat, blood pressure, blood sugar, and blood flow to muscles
- governs action

PARASYMPATHETIC NERVOUS SYSTEM

- conserves and restores the energy stores of the organism
- relaxes the muscles
- decreases heart-rate and blood pressure
- encourages processes such as digestion and elimination

We tend to approach everything from a linear, rational standpoint asking, "How do I get from here to there?" or "What is the proper sequence of steps?"

The dominant use of linear thought reflects a human tendency toward structure: a need for definition, cognition, control, and emotional safety. This tendency promotes a value system that often regards financial and material success as primary to happiness. Our educational system simply reflects and supports this hierarchy by focusing on the development of verbal, linear skills that serve this structure.

The Verbal Approach

There has been an increasingly severe de-emphasis of the creative arts in the classroom. Many art classes stress replication rather than creativity or imagination. Expressive movement is secondary to calisthenics and sports, and the school theater department would rather present a scripted show than originate something through improvisation. Training in abstract thinking, (such as is necessary in algebra and advanced mathematics), memorization of words and facts, and the basic lack of involvement of sensory awareness or emotional response, all contribute to a lopsided verbal or left-brain approach to learning.

If the music educator does not help the student to build right-brain skills while learning the instrument, no matter how the material is presented, it will be processed in a verbal, left-brain manner! In addition, if the music teacher has not developed right-hemisphere skills in balance with left, he/she will actually tend to encourage a left-brain relationship to music through the way he/she communicates about technique and music.

The classic left-brain approach to music tends to encourage learning technique through the use of a system that emphasizes the mindless repetition of proper body moves triggered by symbols on paper or verbal command. While some of this type of learning activity can be useful in moderation, interacting with one's instrument from sensory awareness and emotional expressiveness is often ignored, as are right-hemisphere imagistic skills.

Music is the one language we have that is not a symbol for anything else. Speech and writing are symbols for ideas, places, people and events. Music is music. A verbal approach to music encourages the musician to describe, rather than originate from our own individuality. It trains us to think the music rather than to hear, image, and feel it.

Thomas Blakeslee, in his book *The Right Brain*, describes a Columbia University study in which the left-right hemispheric activity of an audience was monitored during a concert. Sadly, the musically educated listeners showed a right ear advantage (the sign of increased left-hemispheric activity) while the untrained listeners showed a left ear advantage. In addition, studies of the brain-damaged have revealed cases in which instrumentalists with right-hemisphere damage can't remember how to play, yet when sheet music is placed before them, can suddenly and miraculously play their instruments perfectly — only as long as the sheet music remains! (The ability to read sheet music, like the ability to read the words in a book, is governed by the left brain.) These studies reflect the inadequacies of our left-brain oriented music education system.

Left-Brain Effect on Sensory Awareness

When left-hemisphere functions are relied upon to create music, sensory awareness, obviously an essential ingredient in playing any instrument, tends to be dulled or deadened, opening the way for injury.

This occurs for four basic reasons:

1. Going from playing exclusively from sheet music to memorization — sometimes where the player is even "seeing" the printed music in his or her mind's eye — dulls sensory awareness due to the fact that when the eyes are in use, our other senses function at about 20%!

2. The left-hemisphere tends to activate the sympathetic nervous system, increasing the body's oxygen and energy consumption. Blood pressure and blood flow are also increased, and muscular contraction is triggered. The body is, in a sense, on red alert; this is not the time to be relaxed, sensitive or tuned-in!

3. We tend to breathe more shallowly when verbal thought processes are used, yet this is just the time that we need an increase in oxygen intake.

4. The right hemisphere, which tends to influence the parasympathetic nervous system in a positive manner, is not operating enough to facilitate full integration, relaxation, and restoration.

The Right Hemisphere

Looking at a culture such as that of the Australian Aborigine, which seems to rely on and develop the right hemisphere more than the left, provides an interesting illustration of the right/left dichotomy. Thomas Blakeslee describes how, when integrated into white, left-brain oriented schools, the Aborigine children were labeled as having a low I.Q. Yet in an experimental right-hemisphere test situation, they outranked the white children.

The Aborigine children had close to perfect detailed recall of a large number of objects placed before them, viewed only for twenty to thirty seconds. The white children could recall few of the objects, and without details. The results would probably have been reversed if both test groups had been asked to memorize a written list of the objects.

Words (left brain) are fragmented symbols; pictures (right brain) are the whole story. The whole story includes quality of experience, what does what when, speed, intensity, and a plethora of other details. As you begin to assimilate this information, you can see that many of the right-hemisphere driven skills ignored during music education (as well as skills that come from heightened sensory awareness), are extremely necessary to technique and musicianship:

- auditory/tactile

- imagistic

- spatial

- kinesthetic

- ability to process simultaneous sensory input

Additionally, because the right hemisphere seems to trigger the parasympathetic nervous system more effectively than the left, greater relaxation can be accessed more easily. Ideal training, then, would consist of an equal development of right-hemisphere facility in balance with and parallel to left-hemisphere facility. In this next section, *Six-Fold Memory*, we will examine the components of a balanced educational approach.

Six-Fold Memory

In 1986, after I'd given a clinic at Berklee College of Music in Boston, a violin student approached me requesting a private lesson and complaining of problems in performance. At his lesson he played beautifully and as we talked, his problem seemed to be one of memory loss rather than technical or musical difficulties. He said that he'd built up such fear over forgetting the music that he was struggling with stage fright as well.

I decided to explore the subject as much as possible and began questioning him about the nature of his concert preparation. In analyzing his physical and mental preparation in combination with that of a number of subsequent students, a pattern emerged providing useful and interesting information. I began to see why I had been able to shift my own performance experience since I'd started developing a right-hemisphere approach to music.

One product of the therapeutic age is the tendency when someone says they're afraid of something, to think that they have a "neurosis," that their fear is unfounded. The emphasis is then placed on getting rid of the fear, overcoming it, living with it, etc. What if the fear is founded, though? What if it is the product of reality? The person is afraid of something because they don't in fact have the skills to handle it? Interestingly enough, I have rarely encountered a student who had reason to be confident on stage.

Concert performance is generally left to random preparation. In the learning process, we're encouraged to play the piece numerous times and to "memorize" it. Occasionally, when told to iron out the problem passages, we're given technical tips as to the most effective practice habits to accomplish this. Most of the time, though, we're given little or no valuable input as to how to best learn the piece.

The emphasis is usually placed on product rather than preparation. Repetition is offered as our most valuable tool. We then step out onto stage with a kind of moth-eaten patchwork quilt as our support structure, challenged additionally by the psychological dynamic of performance.

The following is a six-fold approach to learning music that provides solid foundation for performance:

Muscle Memory

Commonly used by musicians but often not backed up solidly enough with other skills, muscle memory utilizes the body's ability, developed through insistent (and often mindless) repetition, to perform a series of moves with little or no conscious direction from the mind other than whatever is required to get started. Muscle memory enables us to build levels of technique based on the natural retention of simpler levels of skill. Not backed up with proper mind-to-body foundation, muscle memory on its own doesn't hold up well under performance conditions.

(See *Muscle Memory* unit for greater detail.)

Imagistic Memory

Often overlooked, imaging is a very important element in creating solid technical foundation. Imaging is the ability, with eyes open or closed, to play an entire piece of music in detail mentally.

When you image kinesthetic movement and sound without moving your body you are developing a keen experiential, sensory, sequential, spatial and auditory relationship to the music. It also prepares the mind-to-body hook-up so that the command center is where it should be: in the mind, not the hands!

(See *Visualization and the Imagistic Mind* unit.)

Visualization

Using the mind's ability to create pictures, visualization gives you a more objective picture of your performance much the way an athlete might watch a mental movie of him or herself running and jumping over a six-foot bar. You can practice seeing a mental movie of yourself performing fluidly, effortlessly, expressively, fully aligned and confident. This can be very useful when preparing for performance because you can picture yourself performing in this way in front of a live audience.

(See *Visualization and the Imagistic Mind* unit.)

Auditory Memory

The driving force behind music, auditory memory is the ability to hear the entire piece in your inner ear without referring to your instrument or sheet music. It's surprising how many musicians, when asked to hum or whistle the piece of music they're working on have difficulty hearing the piece in their inner ear!

(See *Auditory Memory* unit.)

Visual Memory

Visual memory is part of the interpretive artist's foundation since most of the music is derived from a written source. Visual memory is the ability to "see" the printed page like a photograph, without physically looking at it. It can be used to trigger sequential (left-brain) memory or be used like a mental cue card.

I don't recommend developing this skill beyond a gentle background presence as it detracts from auditory and sensory awareness. If you have overdeveloped your visual memory, try taping yourself while sight-reading the piece, and then put the sheet music away. Learn the music by playing in unison with the tape. This will help break your visual learning habit.

Since most of us have well developed — if not overdeveloped — visual memories, I have not included a separate unit on it in this book.

Analytical Memory

This approach requires structural analysis (left-brain) of the music, objectively determining the construction, sequence, and names of the notes. Start with the simplest details, such as the key and time signature; learn the modulations and shapes of phrases as well as larger constructs within the whole.

Recognizing internal relationships simplifies the learning process. There is no longer the tendency to think of each note or phrase as a separate entity to be memorized.

Analytic memory calls for a conscious use of theory, intervals, keys, and various scale types.

(See *Analytical Memory* unit.)

SUGGESTED APPROACH

Use the appropriate units in this next section for a detailed description and training approach.

MUSCLE MEMORY

Our muscles, in conjunction with our nervous system, in many ways operate in a similar manner to a computer. We enter information in the form of hundreds of subtle yet very specific micro-movements. Once the entry is completely registered, our hands can actually play a piece of music or, in the case of an improviser, mindlessly run off finger patterns in various keys; all the while we can be thinking about what to have for dinner!

Muscle memory potentially frees us to place our focus elsewhere. We don't have to keep "reinventing" our technique and can increase our technical capacity by layering in information. In a strange way, our fingers, hands and lips can become entirely disassociated from body and mind. It's possible to give them so much power that we're able to go on a mental vacation leaving them to carry on!

In a 1978 interview, a famous musician boasted that he had achieved technical mastery by playing troublesome passages again and again for the duration of TV movies (with the sound turned down). Interestingly enough, his audience described him as a technical wizard but lacking in heart and soul.

While it is commonplace to use repetition to learn a piece of music, this approach causes problems. There is a strong tendency to ignore one's body and its communications regarding muscle tension. In addition, you are training your nervous system to execute movement patterns without any input regarding quality of experience, sensory awareness, breathing, or imaging.

The mind triggers all movement.* To train one's hands without a mind-to-body connection actually takes longer and doesn't always provide a foundation strong enough to hold up under performance conditions.

When you step into performance your body comes alive; your heart rate increases and your adrenaline turns ON. Your body may suddenly feel like the enemy be-cause it demands to be present. Chances are that you will tend to try to play the music the way you practiced it, hoping to feel the way you did in your practice room at home. The struggle to recapture the past can turn the performance into pure misery. Under this kind of pressure, muscle memory will tend to be less available.

You may desperately try to help yourself, but if your preparation is fragmented and incomplete, you'll lack the mental resources that could rescue you. A mind can't remember what it didn't learn in the first place! You could spend the whole concert trying to deaden your body or get away from this intense level of aliveness just to be able to re-access muscle memory.

It's to your benefit, while practicing, to image the notes first, allowing your finger or lip movement to originate in your mind. Muscle memory will still record all of the finger/mouth patterns, but now it will be hooked up to the control center instead of operating independently.

While practicing, the information you program in to your hands can encompass conscious choices about relaxation, the desired auditory/physical interconnection, physical aliveness through deep breathing and sensory awareness, and anything else you would like to include. You can also spend time visualizing yourself playing as if in performance with all of these dynamics in operation. Actually see yourself able to access this wholistic hookup in a fluid and masterful manner.

This kind of preparation for performance creates a body-mind relationship that enables you to make quality of experience choices and follow through on them at will.

When you are fully present and conscious during preparation, you are using nature's own labor-saving device — muscle memory — consciously, which in turn enables you to economize effort in the long run.

---

*Except in the case of reflexive motor responses, such as when the nerve endings signal the body to rebound from a hot object.

■ Use your imagistic mind to originate all finger movement. See/feel/hear the notes before you finger them.

■ Think through what kind of experience and level of expertise you want to have in performance in a detailed manner; assess your practice habits and notice whether there is a discrepancy between the desired result and your manner of preparation; if there is one, adjust your practice time so that it embodies and prepares you for the kind of performance experience you want.

■ Tape yourself while working on a piece of music. Then take a break during which you relax and consciously breathe slowly and deeply. Now listen to the tape and notice what happens to your breathing, muscles, and mind as you listen.

(Assume that your body is remembering and replaying what actually happened when you actively played the music. Take note of the details, such as "my left hand tightened when I heard the third phrase," or "I held my breath while listening to the faster passage." Then go back to the music and play through those sections again, while consciously including whatever was missing the first time: breathe deeply during the fast passage, relax your hands when you get to the third phrase, and so on.)

■ You can also try miming in unison while listening to the tape, moving and staying alive in your body the way you would like it to be when actually playing. Even exaggerate your movement into a dance: the kind of movement that would communicate the music to a deaf person!

■ Whenever you start to worry or fear the worst, picture how you want it to be as if you have already given your best performance and are now remembering what it sounded and felt like.

VISUALIZATION AND THE IMAGISTIC MIND

Using the right hemisphere, we can create mental pictures of any activity in which we are involved. This skill is usually referred to as visualization and has been actively publicized as a tool utilized for manifesting results by athletes, businessmen, and the general public.

The reason that we will be using the term "imagistic mind" in addition to the term visualization is to distinguish between a visual picture of something and a sensorial image.

For instance, you can visualize playing a piece of music as if watching a movie of yourself, or you can experientially image playing that same piece of music with all of your senses. This kind of image is similar to dreaming in that you can experience it as if it were so, even though you are not moving your physical body.

While imaging, you may discover gaps in your knowledge of your instrument or the music. This is useful information; the passages that you cannot image are the passages that you don't actually know. You might have been relying on only one skill, such as sight-reading or muscle memory, to get by.

You can also use imaging to approach your instrument or a particular piece of music in a new way. For instance, you may have learned a piece that expresses the fluidity of water but never considered including a sensory experience of that water-like movement in your body as part of your preparation. Using an image that your body is made of water will change how you sound as well as how you feel. While the left hemisphere tends to maintain a step-by-step, "one thing at a time" style of focus, the power of one's imagistic mind lies in the ability to create a hologram. This hologram enables you to access all of your skills and intentions simultaneously.

Visualization, on the other hand, can be used to help prepare you for performance, and in particular, for television or video performance. To visualize, create in your mind a movie of the performance as if you were sitting in a movie theater and watching yourself on screen.

Through visualization your practice time can become much more focused because you will see the performance as a whole, thereby heightening your awareness of necessary adjustments in the way you use your body or express the material.

A tip to those of you who focus on your worst performance fears: you are actually programming your body/mind to do whatever you picture while worrying.

SUGGESTED APPROACH

■ Using the *Constructive Rest Position* (see GLOSSARY) or an equally comfortable position, begin by breathing deeply and relaxing; then focus on a piece of music and start by playing it very slowly in your imagistic mind. Keep checking your breathing and muscle relaxation. If you find yourself tensing, take a moment and relax again and then try that section again.

■ Use some of the techniques from the *Sensory Awareness* unit to change the way you are "wearing" your body. For instance, imagine that your body is weightless and as flexible as soft rubber. Image playing the music with this new body. Or choose a trouble spot in the music and become someone famous as you play it.

■ Visualize a movie of yourself:

playing while flying

playing an instrument made of feathers

playing with a giant's hand

■ Use these same images but this time use your imagistic mind to feel and experience them.

The above are only suggestions. Experiment and find out what images are most effective for you.

AUDITORY MEMORY

To understand the meaning of creating an auditory image, one has only to think of Beethoven, who composed some of his greatest works after going deaf. He heard the music in his "inner ear" and translated it into written symbols. The auditory image is the genesis of all sound; the optimum level of musicianship is to hear the pitch, phrase, or musical quality and translate it into physical micro-movements. The aural image is then externalized through the instrument, and into the surrounding space and "outer ears" of the audience.

A verbal approach to playing tends to deaden the inner ear. The musician, rather than hearing the music, is either thinking about proper body moves or translating symbols from paper to movement. Hands trained through rigorous repetition to move automatically in a sequential pattern take over. The effect is the same: the musician is hearing the sound after the fact, rather than before.

SUGGESTED APPROACH

■ Practice whistling or humming through the music before playing it, or alternate back and forth between humming and playing. Make sure you can do this without referring to sheet music.

■ Try learning written music by taping yourself playing the piece (slowly) and then close the sheet music and learn the piece by ear from the tape.

■ Play a piece of music slowly, barely touching the keys/strings, so that you are only generating a ghost of a sound (see *Waterbugs and Spiderfingers*). Practice creating the full sound in your auditory imagination, making sure that all physical movement emanates from your inner ear.

■ Play a piece of music slowly but audibly, once again originating all sound from your inner ear. Stop playing every few measures or moments but continue to hear the music in your inner ear, coming back in a few measures later and then dropping out again. When you come back in, make sure it is on the notes or the part of the improvisation that you have moved on to. It's almost as if your inner ear is a piano roll: once the piece starts it doesn't stop until it's over, while your arms and hands occasionally externalize the music on your instrument.

ANALYTICAL MEMORY

When approaching a piece analytically, examine the structural interrelationships. It's amazing how often obvious elements, such as the time and key signatures, are overlooked. Basic structures, such as diatonic (scale-like) movement, key changes, arpeggiated movement (1-3-5 or 5-3-1), and interval relationships are also frequently overlooked, yet these are all critical to solid memory foundation.

If you're an improviser, examining the interrelationships of the chord changes rather than simply memorizing them can solidify your knowledge of the tune dramatically.

Even if nervousness wipes out muscle and auditory memory, you will be able to remember and play the music well by having a clear understanding of the structural elements that constitute the piece.

SUGGESTED APPROACH

Example:

Notice how this melody starts on the tonic, and moves through the notes of a major seventh chord, leading up to the octave, back down to the seventh and then down a major third, only to land on the third of the key. The accompanying chords stay on the tonic, outlining the melody. The entire figure then repeats itself a half step higher, but resolves on its tonic rather than coming down to the three. Then the figure ends back in the original key. Imagine how much harder it would be to memorize this figure note by note!

YOU ARE YOUR INSTRUMENT

New Approaches

SENSORY AWARENESS

The traditional approach to practice has often inadvertently guided the student to pay attention to playing the notes correctly to the exclusion of all else. Unfortunately, this training process creates great technicians who can't feel or enjoy the act of creating music or the music itself.

Early in my experimentation with the relationship between sensory awareness and music-making, a student came to me to learn how to improvise. No matter what I taught her about improvisation, she maintained a mechanical, technically perfect approach to playing. While she was meticulous and highly advanced technically, and her phrasing was filled with carefully worked out dynamics, there was something missing from both her sound and experience while playing.

When I asked her how she felt about music, she talked about discipline and the responsibility of the musician to play well. Teaching her the 12-bar blues didn't help because she approached it the same way she did classical music and I didn't dare bring up jazz chord changes because I knew that she would approach them mechanically as well. In her fifth lesson, I asked her to picture a landscape; to smell, feel, see, and hear the landscape, and to play a piece of classical music while focused exclusively on the landscape.

Suddenly, as if by magic, her playing transformed. Her body moved with great sensitivity and awareness; her sound flowered into an emotionally moving odyssey, and a distinct landscape came into my mind.

This experience was deeply moving for her. She had rediscovered, at long last, her heart connection to music.

Opening one's total sensory awareness takes practice. Start simply by focusing on one of the senses. For instance: increase your awareness of your sense of touch by tickling your skin with a feather or feeling the air "touch" your skin; focus totally on listening to every detail of sound around you while sitting quietly. Notice how an increase in sensitivity to touch and sound makes it easier to open up your whole field of awareness. Focus acts much like a volume switch. As you consciously focus on feeling or listening, you are "turning up the volume" in those areas of your awareness.

Heightening sensory awareness prevents you from causing injury to your body and increases enjoyment of the physical experience of playing music. You can then create a musical experience more akin to dancing or love-making.

■ Play a piece of music while focusing on a particular sense, using an image to stimulate that sense:

Imagine a distinctive smell as you play, allowing the music to actually carry that smell out into the surrounding room. (Some smells are easier to work with than others. Experiment and find out what works for you.)

Imagine that you are tasting something as you play and fill the room with that taste.

Become aware of the air touching your skin and pretend that the air is water or a cocoon. Savor every movement as if you were being stroked by a loving environment.

Imagine that you are breathing in a color that is filling your entire body, moving through your hands into your instrument and filling the entire space around you.

■ Another approach to opening up sensory awareness is to use sensory images that directly affect the way you move, hold or play your instrument.

Imagine that:

Your instrument is made of soft rubber.

Your fingers are ten inches long.

Your instrument is a newborn baby.

Your ears are the size of an elephant's ears.

■ Focus on a particular emotion and allow the music to flow from that emotion. Let your sound truly reflect it, even if your technique changes or your sound doesn't reflect your ideal "in public" tone. You can always make adjustments later.

You can invent numerous sensory and emotional images to work with during your daily practice, including becoming someone else: someone you know, a famous musician, or a prototype of a character. You will notice that as you successfully create these images, your ability to focus will increase, as well as your presence in your body. A sense of integration will occur. This integration will contribute to an overall feeling of well-being, relaxation, physical fluidity, and health.

Natural Biofeedback

For years, I wanted to find someone who could install a pressure-sensitive fingerboard onto a violin attached to a meter that could register the amount of finger pressure used. 99% of the students I'd worked with were using enormous amounts of finger pressure to accomplish something that required far less. They were also complaining to me that their fingers weren't strong enough.

I decided to try something new one day while working with a student who simply couldn't relax his fingers while playing. I asked him to imagine that he was playing on a pressure-sensitive fingerboard, and to assume that his normal finger pressure created a reading of about 80, and that 25 was all he needed to create a full and beautiful tone. I had him create 0 on up to 100 to master the range, and then asked him to create 25 first on one note, then a phrase, and then an entire piece.

It was surprising how easily he used this image to create results that had seemed out of reach for so long. I also discovered, after some experimentation, that when the hands, fingers, and vocal cords are utilized in a relaxed manner, strength and stamina are rarely an issue. Only the musician who is at war with his or her body, forever exerting and pushing it to the limit, feels weak.

In addition, string players increase their ability to play in tune when the muscles are relaxed. Minute pitch adjustment is close to impossible when the fingers are clamped down onto the fingerboard with extreme tension and rigidity.

Imagine that the particular area of your body you want to relax is attached to a monitor showing exactly how much pressure you are exerting. Assume that the needle is close to or inside of the red zone and gradually reduce pressure/tension until you've found zero. Zero is usually indicated by harmonics, air sounds, or barely decipherable pitch, depending upon your instrument.

At zero, it should feel as though you are playing/singing a lullaby through a loudspeaker to an ant! At this point, add in only enough finger and/or arm weight or released breath (use a yawn or sigh to help get in touch with what that feels like) to get a clear sound, but no more. Do this entire process very slowly so that tension is not displaced to some other area of the body.

Waterbugs and Spiderfingers:

Try using the concept that your strings/keys have hairs on them, much like the cilia of the inner ear. Try practicing an entire piece "touching the hairs" of the notes; in other words, use exactly the same finger-placement and timing, but touching only the "hairs" of the notes. Since there will be little or no sound feedback, you'll be utilizing your auditory imaging process.

Now try repeating the piece of music with slightly more finger/arm weight (or breath) and then slightly more, until you have clear tone again.

You will find that as you play with clear tone (keeping the natural biofeedback needle at 25 rather than the ordinary 50 to 90), your fingers will feel more and more like waterbugs walking on water; they'll dance with the lightness that a spider has when it walks across a clear surface.

Singers: Many singers tend to sing too loudly or push too hard, particularly when learning new material or practicing. It's much better to sing new material softly, allowing the desired volume to blossom naturally. In order for you to create this same sensation, you must sing as softly as possible yet still resonantly (not using a breathy sound). You can also practice "giving your weight to gravity" so that you learn to sing from release rather than from tension. (See Tennis Balls in the GLOSSARY for more information.)

WEIGHT AND WEIGHTLESSNESS

When we learn to play an instrument our teachers show us the "correct" way to hold it as well as how to stand or sit. There is an overwhelming tendency to try to maintain that correct position at all times. This restricts sensory awareness, feedback from the muscles, and oxygen intake. The strenuous demands of playing the music well, in combination with a static posture, do not support a quality experience, the optimum use of the body, or the creation of beautifully fluid music.

To create a free and easy dance with your instrument, and as little muscular fatigue as possible, utilize the "weightless" orientation: learn to use gravity, allowing it to do some of your work for you rather than trying to do everything with muscle power; maintain a state of constant subtle movement, in which you are continually redistributing body weight, however imperceptibly; train yourself to consciously release your muscles as you exhale the breath, until you learn how to release consistently, independent of your breathing patterns.

The Use of Gravity

If you have ever tried to lift someone who has been lying in bed sick, you'll remember how incredibly heavy their body was. It could have actually weighed only ninety pounds but felt like two hundred!

Playing an instrument can be a give and take with gravity in which you are constantly releasing your arms and fingers to gravity to create control and mastery over your instrument. Many players overwork their muscles by resisting gravity, contracting and forcing. This is a catch-22 situation. The greater the effort, the harder you must work. When your muscles are contracted, the tension will tend to stiffen your arms. This in turn will give you less natural arm weight to work with, and cause a softer or less lyrical sound quality. In this situation, without knowing how to relax arm muscles into gravity, the musician will tend to press harder.

If you "give" your sound to the room and consciously release arm and finger weight or breath into gravity, you can create volume through resonance rather than muscle. Instrumentalists, make sure that you accentuate horizontal (or vertical, as the case may be) motion as you give to gravity so that you don't get bogged down, and singers/wind players, release your breath as if on a sigh.

Distribution of Weight

One hundred incorrect positions are better than one "right" one.

Whether you are playing a stationary or moveable instrument or singing, it is imperative to incorporate constant, subtle "whole-body" movement so that body weight (and instrument weight) is constantly being redistributed in space and muscles are kept flexible.

Strain and fatigue are often caused by rigidity. The more you allow your body to move and breathe, the greater your stamina.

Arms

Using muscle power, raise your arms straight out in front of you and up to the ceiling, and then lower them to your sides.

Now try swinging them by releasing them to gravity, so they move in a pendulum-like motion. Notice the difference. When you swing freely, giving to gravity, you will find your breath flowing naturally and your movement effortless.

Go back to your instrument and try playing while releasing arm weight to gravity. Experiment with technically demanding passages using the concept of release versus control. The *Pendulum Swings* (See GLOSSARY) can be used to access arm relaxation as well.

Fingers

Place your fingertips on a flat surface and try tapping your index finger up and down and up and down quickly, using muscle power to bring the finger down. Actually emphasize that downward motion, still trying to move quickly and repetitively. Notice how your muscles contract, and movement and stamina tend to be limited.

Now repeat this same movement emphasizing a light lift with a fall into gravity on the downward motion. Your speed and stamina should increase.

Now try to apply this awareness to a specific passage on your instrument.

Spine

As we've just discussed in this section, a static position tends to make the body feel heavy and stiff. Use this exercise to create a lighter, more fluid feeling in your body:

Close your eyes and gently begin to move your spine as if it were a snake. Move sensuously and fluidly. Gradually allow that movement to extend into your neck, arms, and legs.

When you have your whole body snaking fluidly and effortlessly, bring that movement with you as you play or sing. Gradually minimize it so that you change from an external and easily perceptible motion to an internal suppleness and fluidity.

Your Body

Muscle Signals

Out of place vertebrae, disc problems, torn cartilage or ligaments, and bursitis are a few of the common structural injuries resulting from excessive or stressful physical activity. Musicians, though, tend to suffer more from problems in the muscles and tendons.

While playing, muscles can be injured through chronic contraction, overuse, improper warm-up, and an imbalance in the muscle groups due to repetitive use of some and underuse of others. Musculotendinous overuse is usually found in the hand, wrist, and forearm and sometimes in the shoulder, depending on the particular demands of the instrument. Remember, every body is different; comparison only produces trouble. There is no right or wrong technique, either. Five different teachers can teach you five different ways to play and each may work magnificently for his or her own physiology but be wrong for you.

Muscle Communication

There are two muscles or two sets of muscles that work together to maintain the balance or posture of any particular body part; as one muscle contracts, its partner lengthens. This action is created through constant and detailed direction from the brain, which selectively excites the targeted muscle fiber to contract or lengthen. To stop movement, the brain inhibits excitatory impulses from reaching the muscle fiber.

There are sensory receptors throughout the body. The degree and kind of information received through these receptors triggers the level of nerve impulse sent by the brain to a given set of muscles. The amount of nerve impulse sent then determines the amount of contraction or release in that muscle.

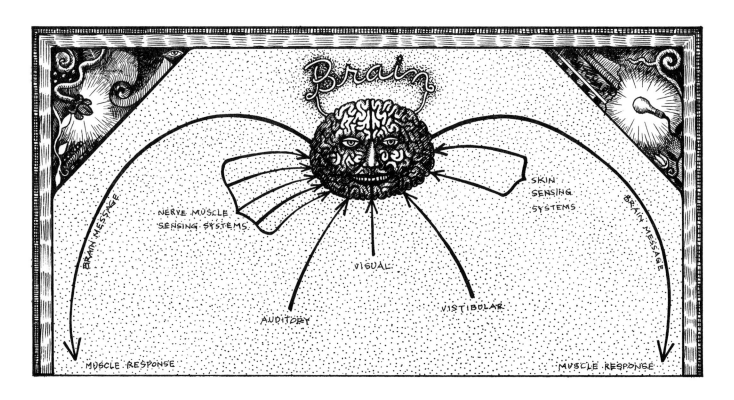

YOU ARE YOUR INSTRUMENT

To be more specific, the brain is constantly integrating an enormous amount of ever-changing information received by five sets of internal nerve-muscle sensing systems, two sets of skin sensing systems, and the auditory, visual, and vestibular sensing systems! The brain then determines the type of communication it will send to the muscles.

Often the body will brace itself in anticipation of unpleasantness by readying important muscle groups for action. This "preparation" isn't always appropriate to the situation. For instance, muscular contraction can easily be triggered by the dynamics involved in performance: fear, anxiety, excitement, to name a few — yet isn't helpful to the performance itself.

Muscles respond to constant, taxing use through a number of sensations: pulsation, burning, slight twinges, a dull ache or soreness, and so on. Sometimes the pain registers in a different area than the actual injury. This is because pain messages in one nerve may cause pain messages in all the nerves along that particular level of the spinal cord.

Sometimes you may feel pain only on the healthy side of the body; muscles that are constantly strained sometimes "speak" less through the language of pain, having learned that complaining does no good. After repeated abuse, such a muscle will often stop relaxing during rest and actually reform into a new, shortened, or knotted shape.

Signs of Injury

Since injury is often incurred as a result of being so focused on the technical aspects of playing that the body is ignored, physical signs may not be evident until after playing, sometimes not showing up until the next day. Symptoms will vary according to the severity of the injury, and can include stiffness, tenderness over the affected muscle-tendon junction, or, more commonly, pain with motion. Occasional swelling may be present.

As the severity of a problem increases, so does the level and duration of pain. Injury from a one-time abuse can heal itself in as little as one to three days. Chronic abuse will yield pain that persists during and after playing. Eventually, if unaddressed, the injury will impair attempts to play.

The Causes of Injury

In addition to ignoring the body while playing, there are a few other factors that may contribute to injury:

■ a new instrument or technical change

■ incoordinated or excessive muscular activity in the technique

■ repetition that is excessive for your particular body

■ forced conformity to a technical approach that is wrong for your body

■ psychological stress (competition, fear, frustration)

■ playing when overtired or run-down

■ failure to take prompt corrective action when warning signals become present

■ extra-curricular activities (e.g. six hours of carpentry before or after practice!)

In their article *Overuse Syndromes in Instrumentalists*, Drs. Richard Lederman and Leonard Calabrese characterize overuse as damage that occurs when a tissue is stressed beyond its anatomical or physiologic limits, either acutely or chronically. They outline five categories of

If muscles are not given relief from tension by relaxation or change of activity, the muscle fibers physiologically 'adapt' to the states of increased tension.

BARBARA BROWN , STRESS AND THE ART OF BIOFEEDBACK

overuse symptoms: "... (1) those involving bones, joints, and bursae, (2) disorders of the musculotendinous unit, (3) primary muscular pain or cramp, (4) nerve entrapment, and (5) the poorly characterized group collectively known as occupational palsies." Pathological changes can include microscopic tears with subsequent swelling or hemorrhage, invasion by inflammatory cells, and ultimately scar formation.

To make matters worse, injury to one muscle may place strain on another, and this can be exacerbated if the musician tries to compensate for injury by placing additional burden on other sets of muscles.

Monitoring Muscle Tension

Pain, as we've discussed, is one of the languages our body uses to communicate. But for accurate information regarding our physical condition, we should not rely on pain alone. There are other ways to monitor your body's condition.

The diaphragm and all surrounding muscles of the stomach and back make it very difficult to breathe deeply when tense. To check your overall level of tension, notice how deep your breath naturally travels into your body. Can you feel it move all the way down into your diaphragm? (It will feel as though it's moving into your stomach/intestinal area.) Or do you feel muscular resistance or tension in your shoulders and upper chest when you try to take a deep breath?

Compare this to how you breathe when you wake up in the morning (before you start thinking about what you have to do!); notice how your breathing changes under stress. Many performers complain of feeling like they can't breathe just before going out on stage. They seem to yawn uncontrollably as they stand in the wings. By the second half of the concert, after they've relaxed into the music, their body temperature has often changed from cold to warm, and their breathing is naturally deeper. (See the unit *Breathing* for more information on the function and mechanics of breathing.)

Another way to check the level of relaxation in your body is to use your fingertips. As you monitor muscular tension through investigation, your fingertips will be teaching your muscles to relax.

To The Touch

To the investigative fingers a healthy muscle has a smooth flat feel, even when well developed. Under pressure it will yield and soften painlessly. Deep pressure will actually feel welcome and be enjoyable.

To The Touch

To the investigative fingers an overtaxed muscle will feel like it has a lump in it or, if the abuse has been constant, can feel like concrete! Certain muscles (such as under the arm) may even feel like harp strings or a cable system. Deep pressure will yield mild to extreme pain. This is a sign of chronic muscle contraction and lactic acid build-up.

To The Touch

Learn how to release the pain when you place finger pressure on the contracted muscle. Exhale fully or even make an open-throated "ah" sound as you press in. This way tension won't be referred elsewhere. The exhalation or sound also helps release the tension.

Learn to notice physical changes while you play; become aware of how your body feels when it is relaxed and flexible. Use the techniques in the GLOSSARY or make up some of your own techniques to integrate a monitoring and adjustment system into your practice time. For example: First I play a scale, then I check and knead my shoulder, then I play a piece, then I breathe deeply in the constructive rest position and so on. As you become more aware of the muscles and muscle groups you have abused, over-used, or not listened to, it will become easier and easier to know what specific techniques to use to keep yourself strong, healthy, and relaxed.

While adjustments in one's technique can ensure that damage will not be caused in the future, this change won't undo any past negative effects on your musculature. This is why, at an Alexander Technique lesson, after the teacher has substantially changed the student's posture, the teacher has only to instruct the student to open their instrument case in order to learn about how they have been using their body during practice. The student's body will immediately and unconsciously begin to assume the shape it associates with music-making!

Our nerves constantly transmit instructions to our muscles. These instructions are always triggered by some kind of thought or feeling. Our muscles remember whatever messages they've received, particularly when those messages have been repeated many times; a *neuromuscular pattern* is formed that associates a particular mental message with a particular physical response. Only activities focused on muscular relaxation, such as professional or self-massage, biofeedback, Gestalt therapy, hot baths, or stretching and strengthening exercises, can release or erase past trauma.

The most dramatic illustration of muscle memory I ever witnessed took place in 1986, while teaching at a weeklong Music for People workshop in New Hampshire. A Canadian musician asked if she could work with me privately, complaining of chronic back pain. Her back muscles were tight, but I could not find anything particularly extreme.

As I worked on her back, I began to ask her questions about her history. At first she could not remember when the back pain had begun. Then we were able to trace it back to the year her mother was in the hospital, dying. Finally, she remembered that her back problems had started after a car accident, but that she hadn't injured her back during the accident.

I asked her where she had been driving the day of the accident. She finally remembered that she had been on her way to see her mother. When asked how she had felt about her mother's illness she became defensive — a healthy sign that we were getting close to something important — but finally admitted that she'd felt sad. I kept reminding her to breathe deeply, and continued to massage her back muscles.

After answering more questions about that period of time, she suddenly began to sob uncontrollably. I call this "when the muscles begin to talk" because I have seen constant evidence that our muscles remember emotional trauma and, if the feelings have not been given full expression, store those feelings. In order for the muscles to relax, those feelings must be remembered and expressed to be released.

It was difficult for her to admit to herself that she had been feeling tremendous anger towards her mother while driving to the hospital. She was actually surprised by these emotions as they surfaced during our session. She realized that she had been angry with her mother for leaving her, for dying. Considering those feelings irrational and unacceptable, she had suppressed them.

I led her in some vocal "sounding" exercises to help express the anger. By the time the session was over, her back muscles were soft to my touch. She wrote me months later to say that she had not experienced any pain in her back since that session.

Not everyone can participate in the process I just described. In the process of healing, as you learn more about your body, you will learn that some types of bodywork may be extremely effective for your best friend, but do nothing for you. We're all different, and it's important to honor our individual needs and preferences.

Some forms of bodywork may produce several days of soreness afterwards. This does not necessarily mean that the work was ineffective. It can mean that the practitioner worked too fast and too deeply for you to absorb. The next time you will be better equipped to communicate your needs. Some people can experience tremendous benefit from deep pressure into the muscles while others will bruise at half that amount!

Always communicate with the health practitioner. If he/she isn't receptive to your needs, then this isn't the right person for you to work with. It can be quite powerful to take charge of your own body and to create an intimate dialogue with yourself on a daily basis. This new relationship will certainly affect other areas of your life and health in a positive and exciting way.

YOU ARE YOUR INSTRUMENT

Breathing

The number of misconceptions among talented instrumentalists, including advanced singers and wind players, regarding how to breathe deeply and the role of breathing in playing an instrument is staggering. Considering that the necessary information is available in any anatomy book, it is a mystery as to how or why there should be such a plethora of misinformation floating around.

We know that breath is essential to life. Let's look at how and why, and in what way proper breathing serves in the creation of music as well as in living a healthy life.

For instance, did you know that a deep breath brings oxygen into the lower section of the lungs, where it enters the blood at a much higher percentage rate than from the upper portion of the lungs? Or that oxygen enables the body to burn food, which is then converted into energy? And that exercise (including playing an instrument) increases the breakdown of nutrients in the system, which in turn increases the production of carbon dioxide, thereby creating a greater need for exhalation, in order to get rid of it?

And did you know that the actual movement of the diaphragm massages the internal organs, including the heart, helping them function on a more optimal level? Or that your brain often uses as much as 20% of the available oxygen in your system? Or that slow, deep breathing initiates chemical antidotes to distress and tension? And best of all, that you can improve stamina and strength by breathing deeply?

Knowing how to breathe correctly is just as much a part of a musician's technique as playing a scale. Let's examine how and why the respiratory system functions the way it does and what you can do to integrate music and breath.

THE MECHANICS OF BREATHING

We have an incredibly cooperative respiratory system designed to filter out dust, bacteria and other life-threatening substances. It is generally better to breathe in through the nose where the tiny hairs called cilia can filter out all pollutants; the nasal passage also warms and humidifies the air so that by the time it reaches the lungs, it is body temperature.

Inhalation takes the air through the nose, the *pharynx* (back of the throat), the *larynx* (voice box), the *trachea* (wind pipe), into two main *bronchi* or *broncheal tubes*.

But why have we lost our natural respiratory rhythm? Isn't it because from the first instant of our lives we hold our breath when we're scared or when we hurt ourselves? Later on we hold our breath to keep ourselves from crying or screaming. Soon we find ourselves blowing out our breath only when we want to express relief.

THE BODY HAS ITS REASONS, THERESE BERTHERAT & CAROL BERNSTEIN

The oxygen then passes through numerous smaller bronchi into over 300 million *alveoli* (air cells similar to the cells or compartments of a honeycomb) in the lungs where each red blood cell has only one second in the pulmonary capillaries to pick up oxygen before returning to the left side of the heart for systematic distribution. The blood transports the oxygen to the body's tissues and picks up the carbon dioxide waste.

Blood flow is greatest at the lowest point in the lungs, where the exchange of carbon dioxide for oxygen takes place between the millions of tiny air sacs and the surrounding network of blood vessels. The carbon dioxide exits on the exhale using the same route as the incoming oxygen. The heart doesn't have to work as hard when you breathe deeply enough to fill the lower lungs, and blood pressure need not then be as high.

When we're not consciously controlling our breath (which is most of the time), the respiratory center has two sources of information that tell the body when and how much to breathe: the degree to which the lungs are stretched and the amount of carbon dioxide in the blood. Based on the information it receives from these sources, the body then signals the main respiratory muscle, the *diaphragm*.

THE DIAPHRAGM

The diaphragm is located just under the lungs, which fill the cavity of the *thorax* (chest) from the *clavicle* (collar bone) down to the twelfth rib. The base of the lungs rests on the top of the diaphragm, which is a curved muscle that spans the base of the ribs and separates the thoracic and the abdominal cavities.

The diaphragm is pierced by the *esophagus*, the *aorta*, and the *inferior vena cava*, one of two principle veins that returns blood from circulation to the right atrium of the heart. The movement of the diaphragm and the inter-

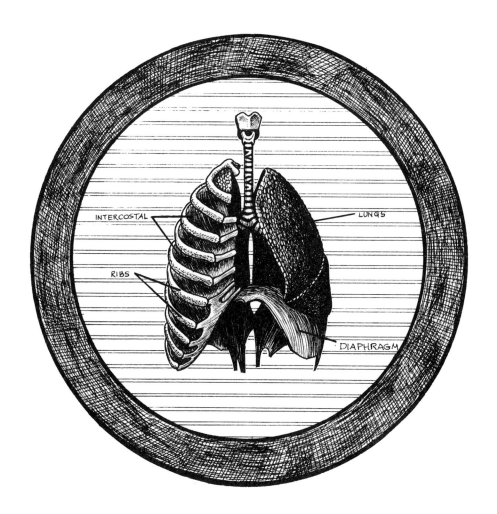

costal rib muscles draws air in like a vacuum. Though expiration can be forced by the intercostal and abdominal muscles, this isn't necessary as expiration occurs naturally through muscular release.

It's quite interesting that the diaphragm, in addition to being attached to the rib cage, is attached to the *pericardial sac* that surrounds the heart, as well as to the *liver*, giving these organs a constant massage. In addition, as the diaphragm sucks air in, it contracts downward, compressing the *peritoneal sac* which contains the abdominal organs.

The blood that is squeezed out of the organs from this contraction returns to the heart much faster, and bile is pressed out of the liver, facilitating its detoxification process. Oxygenated blood may then move into the abdominal cavity.

On a cellular level, respiration takes place every second in over sixty trillion cells throughout the body, as carbon dioxide is exchanged for oxygen. This oxygen, vital to energy production, is also required by each cell in order to carry out its particular unique function.

Energy production without sufficient oxygen is inefficient and entails an unhealthy build-up in the tissues of a substance called *lactic acid*. When your muscles talk to you through the language of pain, the pain is often initiated by the presence of this lactic acid.

METHODS OF BREATHING

Proper breathing can be developed through conscious awareness. In combination with stretching and exercising the muscles, it opens up the blood flow. Toxins are released, nutrients can be brought in, cells are enlivened, cleared up and re-oxygenated, and the internal organs are massaged. What a bargain!

Unfortunately, most individuals breathe shallowly or incorrectly. Shallow breathing supplies less oxygen to the lungs and the individual must now work harder by breathing faster. Chronic shallow breathing promotes a

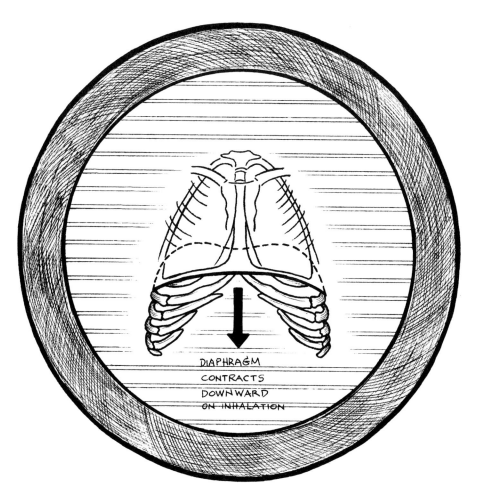

DIAPHRAGM
CONTRACTS
DOWNWARD
ON INHALATION

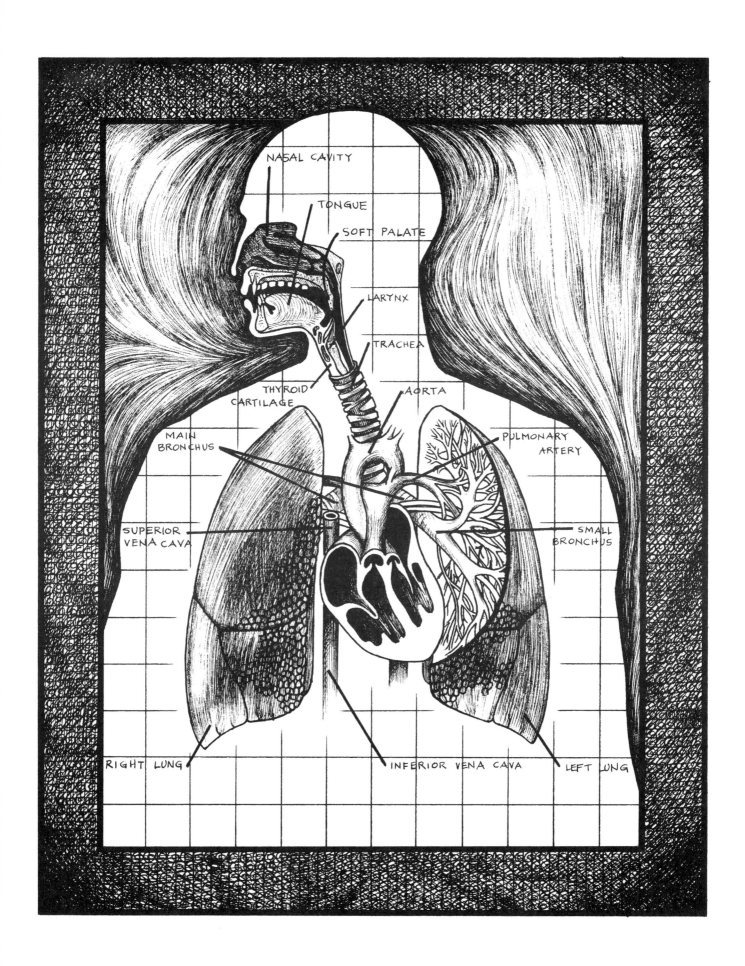

YOU ARE YOUR INSTRUMENT

build-up of carbon dioxide in the system. Since our muscles require constant detoxification (elimination of CO_2 and other waste products) as well as regular supplies of fresh blood carrying oxygen and nutrients, our ability to breathe deeply for the O_2/CO_2 exchange is essential. In addition, the function of deep breathing to facilitate muscular release is of primary consideration to the musician.

At first, proper breathing must be practiced; eventually it becomes automatic. You can start by noticing how you breathe. Trace the movement of the breath into your body. Then begin to direct it into your lower abdomen. Relax the intercostal muscles (located between your ribs) as well as your stomach muscles so that there is a natural expansion in the ribs and abdominal area from the in-breath and contraction from the out-breath. It is usually easier to practice this while lying down with your knees bent. (See *Constructive Rest Position* in GLOSSARY.)

The most important tips to keep in mind are: 1) if your shoulders tighten and raise when you take a deep breath, you're not taking a deep breath! The shoulders should not be involved in breathing at all; and, 2) while the stomach does move in relation to breathing, if you are pushing your stomach muscles out, that too is not the product of a fluidly relaxed, deep breath.

A healthy breath is effortless, naturally expands the rib-cage and presses the organs down and out; it feels like a welcome friend rather than a self-conscious, forced movement. If you have been breathing shallowly, it will take some time for you to learn how to relax your abdominal muscles enough to receive the deep breath naturally.

There are many breathing techniques you can use to enhance your breathing skills. Any breathing exercise is helpful, even one you make up; the more conscious you are of your breath, the less likely you'll be to hold it or breathe shallowly while playing.

Yoga classes are excellent reinforcement for deep, steady breathing. The book, "Take a Deep Breath" (see *Suggested References*), is also an excellent reference.

BREATH AND MUSIC-MAKING

Let's look at what happens when an individual picks up a musical instrument without any breathing awareness or accurate information and coaching available:

To laugh is to breath...

The "serious" lesson molds the student into a constant struggle with mastery. Control and precision over physical micro-movements become all-consuming. Laughter and joy are often absent from this process.

To feel and to move is to breathe...

The harnessing of the body into specialized movements, while maintaining immobility in the "superfluous" body parts, the concentration on motor skill and comprehension of written symbols to the exclusion of quality of experience lead to a closing down of the senses and a tendency to ignore body signals, even to view the body as an adversary that must be controlled and silenced so that it won't get in the way.

To image is to breathe...

Music is generally taught and learned through verbal command: "play softly here," "put your pinky down this way." The left hemisphere of the brain is then constantly exercised and, as we discussed earlier in the unit called *The Brain*, dominant use of the left hemisphere tends to promote irregular breathing.

To express and to communicate is to breathe...

With laughter, tears, joy, sadness — the very expressions of our individuality — excluded from musical development in many subtle and obvious ways, the breathing mechanism closes down, and performance fear takes care of the rest.

EARLY CONDITIONING

Much of our musical training, just like our life training in general, stems from cultural conditioning. To a child, "stop crying" means the same as "hold your breath." "Be quiet" and "stop laughing" also translate into "hold your breath." "Sit still," the shocking reality of adjusting to being in a classroom, means "hold your body rigid and ignore its impulses or communications," which is again equivalent to holding the breath.

There is a basic cultural message that says: "It's okay to be yourself and to listen to your body's impulses in the privacy of your own room, but once in the presence of others you must remember the rules." This comes to the fore when an individual steps out onto the stage.

How can evocative, emotionally resonant, transformational music emanate from suppression and fear — a virtual lifetime of hiding one's expressive self? Only through the miracle of sheer will power! Ironically, it's quite possible that the suffering engendered by fear of performance integrates the individual with his or her own feelings, actually contributing to a more expressive performance.

BREATH AS METAPHOR

The out-breath literally entails a release of the diaphragm and intercostal rib cage muscles. A held breath requires held or contracted muscles. Try holding your breath for a moment right now. Feel what that does to your body. Try to totally relax while holding your breath. You'll find it difficult if not impossible. Now exhale and relax. Feel the difference.

Since the body is one interconnected system, all of the muscles can release with each good deep inhalation/exhalation cycle. With the guidance of conscious thought, this release can be maximized.

I by no means advocate coordinating your physical breath with musical phrasing. This renders dire consequences. I've met musicians who have mistakenly developed the fine art of panting, gasping, or using stop/start long/short breaths parallel to their musical phrases, with the misconception that this aids their technique and musicianship.

I refer more to the art of breath as metaphor. The physical breath moves on a constant, circular, deep in/out cycle, flowing like a river, while the music rolls, undulates, jumps and flies in a parallel motion above the river, always utilizing release rather than contraction to physically create sound. Control, in this new arrangement, is now shifted into a quality of giving, easing, and releasing.

■ Notice how you breathe when you first wake up in the morning, while playing, and while engaged in routine activities in your daily schedule. Don't change anything at first. Just start by noticing and comparing. For instance, what happens to your breathing when you think that you are going to be late, when you're angry, when you're focused on a thought or activity, when you're watching television, and so on.

■ Read and practice the breathing exercises in the book "Take a Deep Breath."

■ Yoga exercises and breathing practices, are very useful in developing and maintaining a healthier breathing mechanism. (See *Yoga* in DIRECTORY.)

Use imaging (see *Visualization and the Imagistic Mind*) to create an experience of yourself playing a difficult passage while breathing deeply.

As You Play:

Imagine that your feet are breathing.

Imagine that your instrument is breathing.

Imagine that each out-breath fills the room with your favorite color.

Imagine that your entire body is breathing in and out, not just your diaphragm.

To practice continuity of breath, utilize sounds ("ah," "oh," long sighs, singing or humming in unison, or lip or tongue trills on long tones) as you play. Since these held sounds are made on the out-breath, you won't be able to hold your breath in; once each breath is used up, your body will automatically inhale.

Practice the *Chest Expansion*, *Pelvic Tilts*, *Trills*, and the *Rib Cage Strengthener* techniques in the GLOSSARY.

The breathing exercises that follow are two of many:

Slow Breath

Lie on your back in the *Constructive Rest Position* and relax. Begin to breathe slowly without forcing. Focus on relaxing your body so that the breath can expand your lower torso without pushing or trying. The rhythm and depth of your breathing should resemble that of a person asleep.

Breath of Fire

Stand or sit cross-legged. Begin to pant through your nose, using short, quick breaths. Emphasize the out-breath, allowing the inhalation to occur naturally.

You will notice your belly moving in response. There should not be much movement in the neck, upper chest or shoulders except that in response to the diaphragmatic movement. If you have difficulty with this technique, try starting on all fours and pant like a dog. Follow each round of fast breathing with several slow, deep breaths. Never force or overdo this exercise.

Awareness and Muscle Balance

INTRODUCTION TO UNITS ON THE BODY

Each unit in the following section addresses one area of the body: its anatomical structure, site-specific problems that are apt to develop during music-making, and suggestions for addressing those problems, or avoiding them in the first place.

Anatomical Structure: Information and illustrations regarding the inner workings of that body part for a clearer understanding of how that area is constructed. This will help you use your body in the most efficient, least stressful manner.

Tendencies: A reference guide stating problems common to the use of that body part.

Suggested Approach: Suggestions for mental and physical healing and balancing techniques.

The final section refers you to the *Muscle Balance Glossary* and the *Directory of Physical and Mental Therapies* for exercises and therapeutic approaches that address the particular problem under discussion. The term "muscle balance" refers to an orientation to the body in which the individual consciously counteracts the chronic single-purpose use of a body part or muscular group with a series of strengthening and healing techniques. This provides muscular and postural support to the over-used area and utilizes the opposing muscle group for balance.

This section is not intended to replace medical care when needed, nor does it address complicated muscular damage. The following information has been designed to help you foster a healthier mind/body interaction during practice and performance. Remember that all types of physical movement, even those requiring energy and shape, can be made from muscular release rather than contraction. The key is to always give body weight to gravity.

Hands and Arms

ANATOMICAL STRUCTURE

The muscles with primary responsibility for movement of the hand are actually located in the forearm. It is crucial to understand this if you are to get optimum use of the hand and arm. Maintaining alignment in the wrist rather than twisting, angling or locking it supports an excellent arm-to-finger interaction. Using the arm and hand outside this natural structural interplay will promote tension and injury.

Notice that the major muscle in the hand is the thumb muscle. It is connected to the pinky muscle. A tight thumb muscle restricts pinky movement and strength.

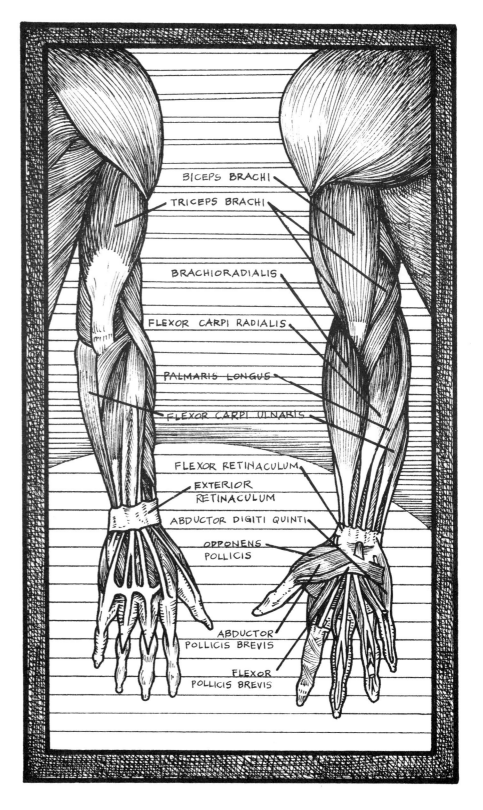

BICEPS BRACHI

TRICEPS BRACHI

BRACHIORADIALIS

FLEXOR CARPI RADIALIS

PALMARIS LONGUS

FLEXOR CARPI ULNARIS

FLEXOR RETINACULUM

EXTERIOR RETINACULUM

ABDUCTOR DIGITI QUINTI

OPPONENS POLLICIS

ABDUCTOR POLLICIS BREVIS

FLEXOR POLLICIS BREVIS

TENDENCIES AND SUGGESTIONS

Contracted thumb muscle while playing:

This pulls the pinky muscle taut, giving the illusion of a weak pinky. Keep thumb muscle soft and relaxed while playing.

Twisted or misaligned wrist:

Angles muscles into a dysfunctional position and places excessive strain on the entire muscle group. Keep wrist aligned and relaxed. If instrument requires a bend in the wrist, be sure to support the action of the hand with how you place and move the arm. Even the intention to maintain connection and energy flow through your arm and hand can make a big difference.

Raised shoulders:

This position overworks the shoulder muscles (*trapezius*) and shoulder blade muscles; it often occurs because of improper arm position in relation to shoulder joint action, or a general lack of body awareness and postural support. Raised shoulders also place stress on the arms and hands. Become aware of your shoulder position as you play; if you discover tension, relax your shoulders down into gravity. See *Freedom Axis* in the GLOSSARY.

Tendinitis or Carpal Tunnel Syndrome

See units titled *Muscle Signals* and *Music Medicine*.

Clenched or locked fingers

Too much pressure and downward motion. Try to move fingers in a more gliding, horizontal motion; use images for release.

Stiff thumb the "morning after":

Excess tension from playing that probably went unnoticed at the time and you are now feeling the result. Become aware of how you use your thumb while playing. Consult the *Natural Biofeedback* unit.

Wrist, forearm and elbow pain:

Excess tension; improper use; excessive repetition; or misalignment. The pain indicates that this has been occurring for longer than any one particular practice period; healing and re-education work are required. See *Tendinitis*.

"Harp strings" under arms:

Excess tension has been allowed to build up in muscles over time. The triceps and biceps need to be massaged; learn how to release your arm weight into gravity while playing.

Shake out your hands and then relax them. Notice that the fingers are gently curved when relaxed, and have their own normal spacing, dependent on knuckle inter-relationship. When you use your hands outside of this normally relaxed shape, you place stress on them. Using your hands with a conscious understanding of their structure will foster healthier finger action and muscle condition.

Monitor your thumb and arm muscles for a build-up of tension; massage them regularly to maintain health in the muscle groups; try incorporating images while you play, such as imagining that your arms are made of rubber.

Strengthen surrounding and interactive muscle groups so that you don't develop an imbalance of overdeveloped muscles partnered with atrophied muscles. Use various arm-lift combinations (offered in aerobic classes), light weights, or isometrics to strengthen the complimentary muscle groups; accompany this with rhythmic deep breathing.

Hand exercises can help develop flexibility and strength. Try "finger ripples" (roll fingers toward palm in a fast ripple: index finger through pinky and then in reverse), and "jelly-fish rolls" (press palm forward while fingers remain pulled back and straight; then allow fingers to relax and curve).

Refer to the units *Natural Biofeedback* and *Weight and Weightlessness*.

Make sure that you support arm use with:

> relaxed shoulders

> aligned spine

> arm/finger movement through release, not contraction

See Also:

MUSCLE BALANCE GLOSSARY

- Arm Lifts
- Arm Shakes
- Freedom Axis
- Hot and Cold
- Imaging
- Pendulum Swings
- Pressure Points for shoulders, arms and hands
- Yoga Arm Stretches

DIRECTORY

- Natural Biofeedback
- Visualization and the Imagistic Mind

The Neck

ANATOMICAL STRUCTURE

Notice how many neck and head muscles there are: muscles to chew, talk, swallow, breathe, move the eyes, nose, cheeks and lips, as well as the head itself. There are more muscles in this small area than in any other section of the body.

Musicians tend to use more muscles to play than they need; the most commonly over-used are the jaw (*risorius*) and neck (*sternocleidomastoid* and *omohyoid*) muscles. There is also a tendency to lock the head into one position and tighten up. Often this position is off-kilter, causing a misalignment of the vertebrae.

Notice that the shoulder muscle (the *trapezius*) extends all the way up the back of the neck and that the *omohyoid* attaches down into the shoulders.

It takes time to learn how to use fewer muscles, and how to relax the weaker outer muscles by using the stronger inner muscles. Begin by noticing what you are doing now.

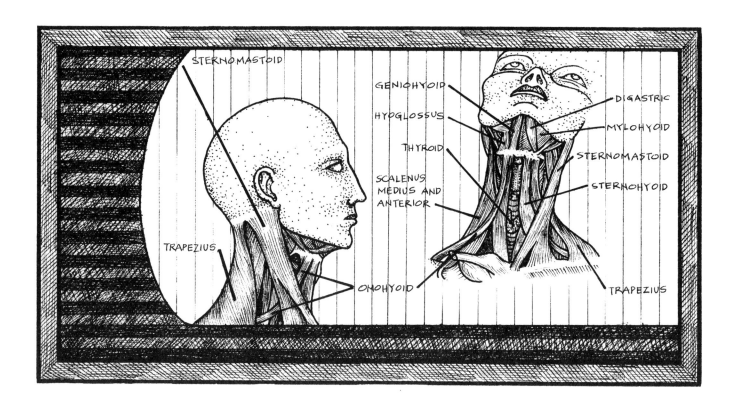

TENDENCIES AND SUGGESTIONS

Headaches:

Can be from neck and shoulder tension or neck vertebrae out of alignment; check head position while playing. Don't be afraid to touch your neck: jiggle, rub, and knead the muscles regularly; get a chiropractic check-up and adjustment; lower intake of sugar, caffeine and refined foods.

Neck pain:

Muscle tension; vertebrae out of alignment. Massage neck regularly; see a chiropractor.

Stiff neck:

Accumulated muscle tension that went unnoticed and unaddressed; can also be caused by extreme temperature changes. Protect neck with a scarf; become more conscious of use of neck while playing.

Sore lips or jaw:

Lack of diaphragmatic support; overuse. Learn how to give lips a good workout without taking them beyond what the tissues and muscles can endure; try shorter practice sessions with rest in between. Support the diaphragm through proper postural alignment; lubricate lips with natural products so that you don't ingest chemicals; use the *Chest Expansion Stretch* and the *Rib Cage Strengthener*.

Facial twitches:

Probably a result of excessive muscular tension allowed to accumulate over time. Be aware of how you use the facial muscles and when you find tension, massage and consciously relax your face. See *Pressure Points* in the GLOSSARY.

SUGGESTED APPROACH

Probe neck muscles with fingers and search for muscles that feel like cables or are hard to the touch. Gently massage these muscles until they soften. You can also try soaking in a hot bath or applying a hot towel compress to your neck to help the muscles relax.

To determine flexibility, gently lean head forward, backward and to each side. Head should be able to go all the way over without pushing or pulling and without pain.

To stretch neck muscles, release head slowly into each of the four positions for several minutes. Relax the weight of the head into gravity, using the exhale of the breathe to help. Don't force or push.

When playing, try to keep head centered; when turned to the side, make sure the head isn't tilted or pulled at an angle. Don't lock your head into one position; use constant subtle, fluid motion, like a tightrope walker.

See Also:

MUSCLE BALANCE GLOSSARY
- Constructive Rest
- Constructive Rest Position
- Head lifts
- Hot and Cold
- Massage
- Neck Stretches
- Pressure Points (neck and shoulders)
- Snaking

DIRECTORY
- Alexander Technique
- Chiropractic

The Shoulders

ANATOMICAL STRUCTURE

Connected to and affected by the neck muscles, the top of the shoulders (the *trapezius* and the *deltoids*) and the area surrounding the shoulder blades (*supraspinatus*, *rhomboid major* and *minor*, *serratus posterior inferior*, and *latissimus dorsi*) are common collection points for tension.

Chronically raised, pushed forward, or twisted shoulders will cause tension and pain. Sometimes it can be a very subtle lift or twist, not visible to the untrained eye.

Shoulder pain can also come from bearing down with the arm muscles while playing. Learn how to release to gravity in your arms and shoulders as you play; make sure you support upper torso activity with an aligned and flexible lower torso.

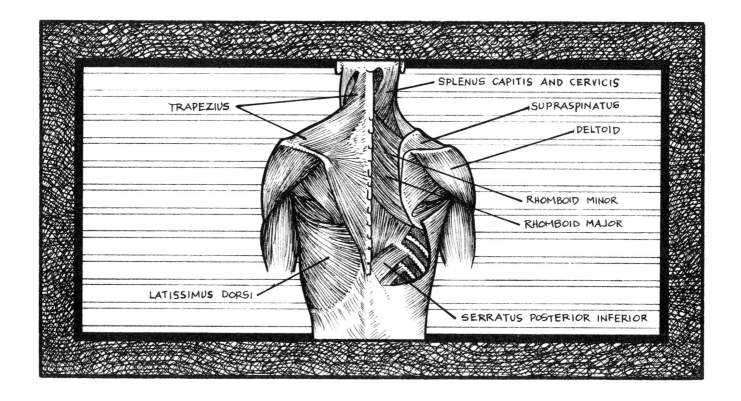

YOU ARE YOUR INSTRUMENT

TENDENCIES AND SUGGESTIONS

Tight, raised shoulders:

Lack of awareness while playing regarding body position and tension. Adjustments may need to be made in the way you hold or interact with your instrument or your position in relationship to the music stand, if you use one.

Curved or rounded shoulders:

Same as above. Muscle balance techniques are required to stretch and strengthen opposite muscle groups and to help build aligned posture.

Strain in shoulder blades:

Holding up arms; bearing down with muscle rather than through a release to gravity. Support arms from lower back more by sitting or standing with proper alignment; release tension regularly by using body work

suggestions in DIRECTORY so that tension doesn't have an opportunity to accumulate.

Shoulder muscles are hard to the touch but don't hurt:

Muscle tension has been chronic and muscles are no longer communicating through the language of pain. Massage or shiatsu can be used to release lactic acid build-up; learn how to release tension on a daily basis.

Twinges in shoulders or under shoulder blades:

Muscles are oscillating between contraction and release; pain or discomfort is their way of telling you that you need to make an adjustment in how you're using them. If you can't make an adjustment in favor of relaxation while playing, then take some time away from the instrument to stretch and massage the muscles so that you can come back to your practice renewed.

SUGGESTED APPROACH

Investigate your shoulders daily with your fingertips to find out what's going on in that area. Test freedom of arm and shoulder movement (see *Shoulder Rolls*). Look at the shoulder area above the collarbone to help determine the degree of muscular contraction in the trapezius muscle. If there is an enormous ridge above the collarbone, then you can assume that you have been tightening the trapezius while playing. The first step is to use mas-

sage or acupressure to release the muscles; once you have diminished the size of the ridge and softened the muscles, then constantly check that area while playing to make sure you stay relaxed. Constantly relax the weight of your arms into gravity to foster greater release.

A long soak in a hot tub can also help the shoulder muscles soften.

See Also:

MUSCLE BALANCE GLOSSARY
- Arm Lifts I and II
- Arm Shakes
- Freedom Axis
- Hot and Cold
- Pendulum Swings
- Shoulder Rolls
- Tennis Balls
- Yoga Arm Stretches

DIRECTORY
- Acupressure or Shiatsu
- Massage

The Upper Torso

ANATOMICAL STRUCTURE

The upper torso contains the lungs and houses the diaphragm in the rib cage. It is an important support center for the arms, neck, and head.

Proper alignment and elasticity contribute to deeper breathing and better support. This is crucial to the oxygenation and strength of the entire body.

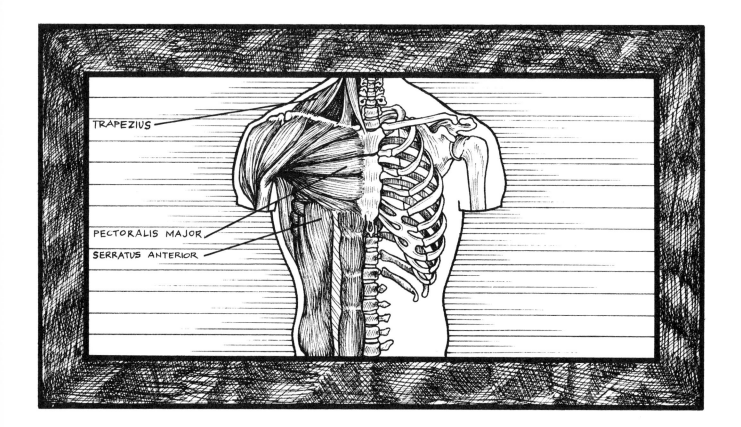

TENDENCIES AND SUGGESTIONS

Collapsed rib cage:

Lack of awareness of posture; pressing shoulders and arms forward too much while playing. Strengthen back and intercostal muscles to help support proper alignment. Use the *Rib Cage Strengthener*, *Chest Expansion*, and *Arm Lifts* techniques.

Shallow breath or breath pressed into lungs and shoulders:

Poor alignment or tension is blocking deep breathing; you may also have a misconception about how to breathe. See unit titled *Breathing*.

Twisted torso position:

Lack of body awareness. Bring instrument to you, don't go to instrument.

Inflexible rib cage:

You are either holding your body rigidly or holding your breath while playing, or both. Use *Snaking* to increase flexibility and connect playing with breathing.

Pain under shoulder blades; arms tire easily:

Release arm weight to gravity rather than bearing down with arm muscle; give arms proper support through postural alignment of the torso. Use the *Chest Expansion* and *Rib Cage Strengthener* techniques as well as the *Constructive Rest Position*.

Difficulty with breath control and stamina, or overworked facial and throat muscles:

You are probably using your facial muscles too much and are not supporting your breath properly with correct posture and correct deep breathing. See *Rib Cage Strengthener* and the unit *Breathing*.

SUGGESTED APPROACH

Focus on developing aligned posture through awareness, exercise, and *Alexander Technique*. Practice deep breathing; use the *Yoga Breath* and the *Rib cage Strengthener* to strengthen and increase diaphragm action.

Read the unit titled *Breathing*.

See Also:

MUSCLE BALANCE GLOSSARY

- Arm lifts
- Chest Expansion
- Constructive Rest Position
- Hang-over
- Rib Cage Strengthener
- Tennis balls
- Yoga Arm Stretches

DIRECTORY

- Alexander Technique
- Yoga

The Lower Torso

ANATOMICAL STRUCTURE

The lower back can be used as a tremendous support system to the arms and shoulders if your posture is aligned.

The lower abdomen, which is considered the power center of the body, or the *Hara* (a term used in Yoga meaning "the seat of bodily energy" because it is the exact point where the upper and lower halves of the body are joined), houses the internal organs. When relaxed, the lower abdomen allows room for a deep inhalation.

Hyperextension of the lower back (tipping the pelvis forward by pointing the pelvic bones towards the floor and pressing back the buttocks) exerts enormous pull on the legs and upper torso; it is a dysfunctional position that makes it hard to breathe deeply or to support your upper torso properly. In addition, lower and/or upper back pain may result.

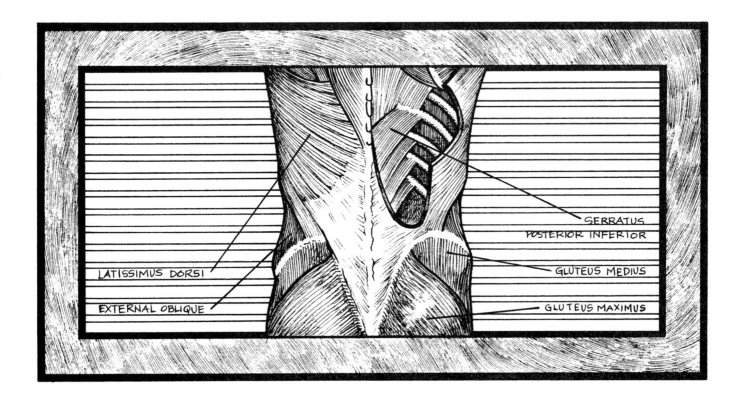

LATISSIMUS DORSI

EXTERNAL OBLIQUE

SERRATUS POSTERIOR INFERIOR

GLUTEUS MEDIUS

GLUTEUS MAXIMUS

TENDENCIES AND SUGGESTIONS

Pain in the groin or down the legs:

Can be caused by a weak, strained, or out of balance psoas muscle; or could be from out-of-place vertebrae. Use *Psoas Balance Technique*. See a chiropractor.

Hyperextension of the back:

This throws your entire body's alignment off and can be changed through flexibility and strengthening exercises. Without attention you will develop back pain and your arms will have to work twice as hard.

Stomach muscles habitually contracted:

This blocks full, deep breaths into the diaphragm. Practice breathing deeply and releasing the stomach muscles. See *Alexander Technique*; read unit on *Breathing*.

Twisting of the hips:

Align your body properly and then bring your instrument to you rather than twisting yourself to go to the instrument. If you must turn, do so with the consent of the hips and support this with your leg position.

SUGGESTED APPROACH

Use a mirror to get a sense of your postural tendencies; keep your knees unlocked and slightly bent to help align your lower back. Never force your body into a new position: learn how to release your muscles into position, and then strengthen them to hold the alignment.

Take a hot bath to help your lower back relax.

Read the unit titled *Breathing*.

See Also:

MUSCLE BALANCE GLOSSARY

- Constructive Rest Position
- Hang-over
- Hula hoops
- Leg lifts
- Pelvic tilts
- Psoas Balance Technique
- Rib Cage Strengthener
- Stomach Strengthener
- Yoga Breath

DIRECTORY

- Alexander Technique
- Yoga

The Legs and Feet

ANATOMICAL STRUCTURE

The support system for the entire body, our legs and feet are often ignored and forced into strange positions; standing on the sides of the feet and putting all of one's weight onto one leg for long periods of time are the most common transgressions.

Many musicians unknowingly tense their leg muscles as they play and later wonder why their legs ache!

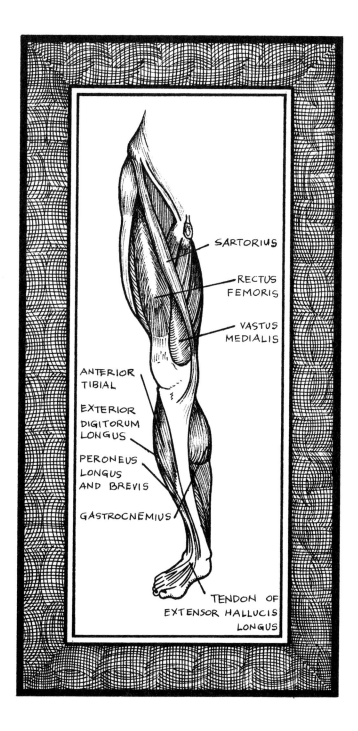

SARTORIUS

RECTUS FEMORIS

VASTUS MEDIALIS

ANTERIOR TIBIAL

EXTERIOR DIGITORUM LONGUS

PERONEUS LONGUS AND BREVIS

GASTROCNEMIUS

TENDON OF EXTENSOR HALLUCIS LONGUS

TENDENCIES AND SUGGESTIONS

Weight on one foot/leg:

This positions the hips unevenly, causing uneven upper back support; it can also throw vertebrae out of alignment. Consciously place your weight on both feet, establishing a firm contact between the bottom of each foot and the floor.

Locked knees or locked hip socket:

You can throw off your entire spinal alignment; keep knees bent and hips flexible.

Tightening of muscles:

Keep checking legs and feet for tension. Avoid locking yourself into one position; use constant subtle movement to help release any tension.

Pins and needles down the leg:

This pain is often referred from lower back problems or the psoas muscle. See *Lower Torso*.

Calf spasms:

Often referred from vertebrae out of alignment in the spine; psoas muscle out of balance; a build-up of tension; or calcium deficiency.

Flexed or angled foot:

Places stress on the legs, the knees, and the hip joints; creates a shaky center of balance and encourages gripping in other support muscles to compensate. Become aware of the position of your feet while playing; if you find yourself angling or flexing a foot, adjust its position so that it is centered.

SUGGESTED APROACH

Keep knees slightly bent while playing. Never go static; always incorporate subtle shifts in weight. Keep legs aligned; don't turn feet in or out to excess.

Lie on your back on the floor and bring your legs above your stomach, knees slightly bent, feet facing the ceiling. Gently shake your legs through a slight kicking action. This will help the muscles to relax.

See Also:

MUSCLE BALANCE GLOSSARY
- Leg Stretches
- Psoas Balance Technique
- Snaking

DIRECTORY
- Acupressure
- Massage
- Shiatsu
- Yoga

The Jaw and Lips

ANATOMICAL STRUCTURE

The jaw and lips are often overworked by wind players and singers through inadequate breath support, general tension, and overuse.

This area can benefit enormously from a properly aligned neck and spine, diaphragm support and strength, and practice sessions that include frequent breaks to rest and relax.

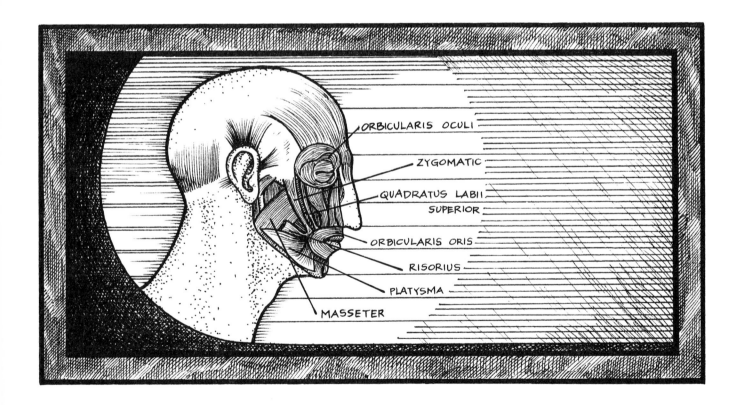

ORBICULARIS OCULI

ZYGOMATIC

QUADRATUS LABII SUPERIOR

ORBICULARIS ORIS

RISORIUS

PLATYSMA

MASSETER

Tendencies and Suggestions

Lack of muscle power:

Chances are good that you're overworking your throat and jaw muscles or aren't giving enough support from the diaphragm and intercostal rib cage muscles. See *Rib Cage Strengthener*. Read "The Contemporary Vocalist" by Jeannie Deva.

Aching jaw:

Same as above. Massage entire area and press into appropriate points. See *Pressure Points* in GLOSSARY and *Temporomandibular Joint Dysfunction* in MEDICAL CONDITIONS.

Sluggish tongue action:

Too much tension or overuse; train yourself to use your tongue from release rather than contraction. Rest and use *Tongue Trills* (see GLOSSARY).

Earaches:

Definitely see a doctor. This can be caused by or exacerbated by pressure from the jaw muscle. Massage the jaw area; press into the appropriate points. See *Pressure Points* in GLOSSARY and *Hearing Loss* in MEDICAL CONDITIONS.

Chapped, cracked, or peeling lips:

Can be caused by long practice sessions without adequate rest in between; another contributing factor is too much strain and effort. Use a natural lip cream so that you don't ingest chemicals.

SUGGESTED APPROACH

Use proper breath support through postural alignment and correct use of the diaphragm. Learn how to release your jaw and tongue muscles during and after practice and performance.

Read unit titled *Breathing*.

See Also:

MUSCLE BALANCE GLOSSARY
- Lip Trills
- Pressure Points for jaw and neck
- Rib Cage Strengthener
- Tongue Trills

DIRECTORY
- Acupressure
- Acupuncture
- Shiatsu

The Standing Musician

The standing musician has all of the problems and challenges of any two-legged creature: maintaining erect posture against the constant pull of gravity while sustaining stamina and fluidity of muscle movement.

There are two particularly important keys to comfort while standing: subtle and constant movement of the entire body to continuously redistribute weight, and keeping one's knees and ankles bent and flexible.

When the body is erect, the back muscles tend to shorten; this tendency is exaggerated when the arms are lifted and held up in the air for periods of time. Keeping the knees slightly bent and using subtle movement to provide a release in the hips helps take stress off of the lower back.

If you wear high heels, the shortening of the muscles of the heel coupled with the angle of the foot will place even more stress on your back, making it imperative to bend your knees and keep moving.

Be sure to check that any rotation of your body occurs at the waist with the "consent" and rotation of the hips, and is supported by the position of the feet. The feet should be aligned under your hips and your weight should be evenly distributed. Rotation of the rib cage while leaving the hips stationary places undue stress on the diaphragm and lower back.

HYPEREXTENSION

Many standing musicians have problems with hyperextension of the lower back. The *Constructive Rest Position* will help realign the spine, as will the bending of the knees. Also use *Pelvic Tilts* (see GLOSSARY) to increase flexibility.

Try to keep your pelvis dropped into place with release rather than through a muscular holding action. To determine your current hip position, locate your hip bones (the small bone that protrudes on either side of your belly). If these bones are pointed downwards, that indicates hyperextension. The optimum placement is in a forward position.

PRONATED KNEES OR FEET

Check that your feet are flat on the floor and aligned while playing. Standing on the insides or outsides of the feet, turning the feet in or out to excess, or allowing the knees to turn in while standing can place undue stress on the legs, hip sockets, and lower back. In addition, a faulty stance robs the body of the support structure it needs. Good footing is particularly crucial for singers and wind players because the movement of the diaphragm can be hampered by improper alignment.

Bend forward as far as you can, and relax, with your arms and head hanging down towards the floor. Breathe deeply to help your back muscles and hamstrings (backs of the legs) stretch and lengthen. Do not lock your knees. Do this every fifteen or twenty minutes when practicing to help counterbalance the effects of standing.

The *Shoulder Stand* and the *Plow*, positions used in Yoga, are excellent for stretching and strengthening the lower back.

See Also:

MUSCLE BALANCE GLOSSARY
- Hula Hoops
- Pelvic Tilts
- Pendulum Swings
- Psoas Balancing Technique
- Rib cage Strengthener
- Snaking

DIRECTORY
- Acupressure
- Acupuncture
- Alexander Technique
- Massage
- Weight Training
- Yoga

The Seated Musician

There are several postural tendencies that contribute to muscular fatigue, pain, and injury when playing a musical instrument while seated. The most common include slouching, leaning back on one's gluteus maximus rather than sitting upright on one's sitz bones, and twisting one's legs and torso in opposite directions.

In addition to contributing to the health of the lower back muscles, correct posture supports efficient shoulder blade and arm movement. The freedom and strength the lower back provides is impaired if the back muscles are collapsed downward or straining to hold your body up.

Many musicians believe that correct posture requires more effort than slouching. This isn't true. The muscles actually have to work harder when the spine isn't aligned. The smaller muscles no longer have the support of the strong muscles that run along the spine.

What you communicate through your posture on stage is another element to consider. Good posture and dynamic alignment tend to communicate greater presence and command.

SUGGESTED APPROACH

Use the *pelvic tilts* (see GLOSSARY) to achieve greater mobility in your pelvic muscles and a clearer picture of the difference between proper and improper position. Practice them while standing, and then try using the same movement in a rolling motion while seated.

Practice lifting your arms as if you had balloons in your armpits; let them float up. Use of this image will help teach you how to lift your arms from your spine, rather than contracting the biceps to pull the arm muscles up.

Always make sure that your feet are in contact with the floor, and your legs are open wide enough to support your body comfortably with minimum effort.

Study the *Alexander Technique* (see DIRECTORY) to learn proper alignment so that there is no undue strain in any one area.

Never practice while lying down in bed or sitting slumped in a chair.

Music Medicine

Music Medicine

THE HEALING PROCESS

It's important, if experiencing frequent or constant pain, to seek medical help. Correct diagnosis will determine the most effective treatment. However, if the use of drugs (in the form of pills or injections) or surgery is recommended before trying rest, physical therapy, and technical/physical adjustments — unless, of course, the injury has reached emergency proportions — seek a second opinion.

Besides the negative side-effects or trauma that drugs and surgery can have on the body, these "solutions" to injury tend to take responsibility away from the individual; instead of learning how to effect physical change and use the body more intelligently, the individual looks for answers outside himself.

Drugs often mask the symptoms, removing the pain or discomfort. The problem with this is that the moment most musicians feel better, they tend to jump right back in where they left off. With no physical or mental re-education, they quickly re-create the same condition, or protect the injured area so much that they cause a problem elsewhere!

Total rest and re-education are generally the keys to recovery. Medical or home treatment can take anywhere from several weeks up to a year depending on the severity of the condition. If you are truly committed to healing your injury and willing to do what it takes to achieve a change, you can generally expect anywhere from major improvement to 100% healing.

The process of healing, the search, is an important learning experience that will certainly help you on your way to total health.

Home Treatment:	Medical Treatment:	Following Treatment:
Rest	Rest	Short Practice Sessions
Body Work	Ice Packs	Warm-up/Cool Down
Exercise	Analgesic anti-inflammatory agents	Postural Training
Technical Adjustments	Nonsteroidal anti-inflammatory drugs	Relaxation Techniques
Visualization	Corticosteroid Injections	
Deep Breathing	Surgery	
Conscious Practice		

The following are important factors in the healing process:

- Strengthening the surrounding muscle groups.

- Proper nutrition.

- Development of conscious release and purposeful movement.

- Knowing when and how to rest.

- Knowing how to deal with certain environmental factors such as volume or competition.

- Knowing how to create a dynamically integrated system (a balance of mental and physical awareness).

Only under emergency conditions (you've ignored the problem so long that you're bordering on permanent damage and need to bring down the inflammation immediately) are drugs crucial or even desirable in the healing process.

Note: Wearing an Ace bandage may force you to rest the injured limb, but it also reduces circulation and may cause edema (swelling). How can the body heal an area that's isolated and frozen? If total rest is absolutely necessary, use a splint rather than an Ace bandage. Just be sure, if your finger, hand, or wrist is in a splint, to massage the upper arm and shoulder on that side. The body will often tense neighboring muscles to protect the injury; this reduces badly needed circulation.

CONSTRUCTIVE REST

There are two kinds of rest. The first simply consists of a reduction of activity. Use the other hand more, ask for help carrying and doing things, use a knapsack rather than a shoulder bag, and so on. To facilitate healing of the irritated connective tissue, rest is crucial. If you have to cancel rehearsals and concerts, do it, or you jeopardize your future.

Continuous use of an already distressed tendon can cripple the area. It may take an emotional adjustment to forego your activities and commitments, but if continuing them means deterioration and repetition of injurious habits, then those commitments, whatever they are, are not worth the cost in the long-run.

I call the second kind of rest constructive rest. This means resting while practicing a healing mental or physical activity. Here are some suggestions:

- Lie down and imagine that the air is your favorite color; breathe the color into your entire body. Send the color into the injured area and permeate every cell with this color.

- Imagine that there are little elves or beings cleaning out the injured area and bringing nutrients in. Pass energy in the form of white light through the top of your head, down through your shoulders and arms, and out your fingertips and palms; keep moving the energy through until you tingle all over.*

- Take a hot bath (or warm — depending on the extent of your injury — see Hot and Cold in GLOSSARY) while listening to soothing music played by an instrument other than your own; focus on breathing deeply and sending healing energy to your injured limb.

- Make up your own visualizations.

The visualization techniques just outlined have two important functions:

1. They actually increase circulation and effect internal relaxation and healing.

2. You are establishing a body/mind connection so that later, when you are playing again, you will have an easier time using your body in exactly the manner you choose.

*When using visualization techniques such as sending white light or energy to an injured area, always make sure that you create a current that moves through the area. Example: For tendinitis in the forearm, move the white light/energy through the top of your head, down your shoulders and arms, and out through your fingertips.

PHYSICAL & TECHNICAL RE-EDUCATION

As has been discussed throughout this book, our physical state of being begins in the mind. A good way to start approaching living in our bodies differently is by exploring some of the old attitudes, definitions, and approaches that helped to create injury in the first place. These can be replaced by new ideas and mental images that will serve the healing process.

There are numerous conventional and nonconventional healers available to help you on your road to health. A medical doctor will give you a clear idea of the existing condition's status; then, approaches such as physical therapy, shiatsu, acupressure, chiropractic, acupuncture, herbology and massage, to name a few, will be useful to you in different ways. Generally, their emphasis is on helping the body heal itself by removing any blocks in energy flow, increasing circulation, and regenerating nerve and muscle tissue.

Use the DIRECTORY at the end of this book to determine a course of action that will help train you in the areas in which you lack skill. Learn how to facilitate a greater mind-to-body interaction so that you are able to relax specific muscles and muscle groups while playing. An activity can be performed either through contraction or release. Learn the difference.

You may need to relearn your repertoire using this new approach since your nervous system probably recorded the old mind/body hook-up as well as the music. Through experimentation you will build a new kind of repertoire — one of healing and relaxation techniques that you can use during and after practice and performance.

CHOOSING A DOCTOR

In addition to expertise in his or her chosen field, it's important that the doctor you choose to work with has a special interest in musicians as patients. Previous experience with musicians increases a physician's understanding of the particular language and problems of the musician.

A good doctor, in addition to a thorough examination, should take a detailed history of your practice and performance habits, note any recent changes in your technique and repertoire, and ask you to pinpoint passages or techniques that are specifically troublesome. It's also important for the doctor to watch you while you play, particularly if your problem occurs only during specific technical activities.

A doctor who asks you questions about your nutritional, psychological, and economic tendencies evidences an awareness that you are a whole person, not just a set of hands or arms.

Treatment must include changes in your practice habits, which may involve adjusting the position of the instrument or altering your technique; this work will obviously require the expertise of a teacher who has body awareness.

If the doctor recommends surgery, get a second opinion. Anti-inflammatory drugs may be necessary, but make sure that you use them cautiously. The overuse of adrenal cortical steroids — which are often used to control inflammation — can actually prevent healing of tissue and may produce atrophy. Some doctors will automatically prescribe anti-inflammatories when rest and an ice-pack may be all that's required.

As was mentioned earlier, steer away from Ace bandages unless absolutely necessary. They're used to help facilitate rest and to "protect" the injury, but they can cause

---

Note: When a muscle or muscle group has been chronically contracted, you may experience enormous pain and/or soreness during and after body work. The muscles are going through a healing process that must be respected. If you do body work, don't play immediately afterwards or jump into vigorous activity. Give yourself time to heal. Treat yourself gently, and give your muscles time to acclimate to a new state of being.

edema (swelling of the outer extremity — for musicians, the hand) and tend to cut off circulation. The body can heal more effectively if it has access to the injury.

One has only to read a few medical case studies to realize that medicine is not always a precise system of diagnosis and cure — particularly Music Medicine, which is such a new field. For instance, one case study cites trying antiparkinsonian, anticholinergic, and tricyclic antidepressant medications as well as transcutaneous nerve stimulation, myotherapy, wrist cock-up splints, and EMG biofeedback on six injured pianists with no positive results. (I won't even speculate on the possible negative side effects or costs of some of those treatments!)

We can, however, learn from these case studies. Each of the recipients had extended his practice sessions prior to injury, after concluding that his technique was insufficient for the piece. Additionally, almost all of them compensated for perceived weakness by using other muscles not designed for that particular activity. By the time they sought medical help, their conditions were fairly well developed, they were desperate for help, and they were probably willing to try anything.

This is obviously a dangerous position in which to place yourself, not only for the degree of physical damage already incurred, but because you will be less likely to take the time to research and choose the doctor who is right for you. The very rationale that contributed to overcompensation during practice — "I must have the results any way I can get them right now" — will probably still be present during the healing process.

Remember that Music Medicine is a relatively new field. No matter how excellent the intentions of the doctor, he/she may not know all of the answers. Experimentation may be required, but make sure you are aware of all of the possible courses of action and are a part of the therapeutic decision-making.

MEDICAL DIAGNOSIS

Depending upon the severity of the injury, the doctor may want to run some tests to gather more specific information. The following are some of the more common tests used to determine the correct diagnosis and healing process for your injury:

Blood Tests

Specific blood tests that reflect evidence of inflammation (the so-called sedimentation rate) or muscle injury (muscle enzymes) may be ordered by physicians. Because many modern labs use automated equipment to test blood, it may actually be cheaper to order an automatic panel, usually referred to as a SMAC, rather than a single blood test. In this case, you may get a computerized printout of your liver function, blood count, blood sugar, and cholesterol, in addition to the specific test results desired. This is good information to have, although it would only rarely apply to the diagnosis of music-related conditions.

EMG (Electromyogram)

EMG measures the nerve conduction velocity (speed of a nerve impulse) by using two electrodes inserted into the skin with fine needles. It's like acupuncture with a hi-tech twist! This is useful to diagnose nerve entrapment syndromes, such as carpal tunnel syndrome. In this case, pressure on the median nerve causes a slowing of conduction velocity which can be seen on the EMG recording. This test is usually done by neurologists and may cost up to several hundred dollars.

MRI (Magnetic Resonance Imaging)

This is a new way of creating images of internal tissues by applying magnetic fields to the body. The pictures are quite striking and can show subtle evidence of muscle injury as well as the presence of any more serious conditions (e.g. tumors). This would only rarely be used to help diagnose playing injuries and is very expensive.

Radiographs are standard x-rays, which are still the best way of diagnosing mild arthritis or other problems involving changes in the bones.

MEDICAL PROBLEMS

It's difficult to come to grips with your physical condition if you're bombarded by incomprehensible medical terms. This glossary provides an overview of the most common injuries sustained by musicians:

Arthritis

Arthritis is an inflammation of a joint. Its symptoms can range from mild stiffness and swelling to pain and severe restriction of movement in the affected area. No one really knows what causes arthritis or how to cure it; sometimes food allergies or extreme tension can contribute to the condition. If, after trying some physical adjustments and body work, pain persists in the same spot every day, see a doctor. Some arthritics have been able to improve the condition through a change in diet (with the avoidance of sugar and the "nightshade" food group in particular) and daily aerobic activity. Anti-inflammatory medication such as aspirin or ibuprofen can be very helpful. Steer away from tylenol or steroid injections.

Arthralgia

Arthralgia refers to a painful joint that is not swollen.

Bursitis

Bursae are synovial-lined sacs (synovia is a transparent lubricating fluid) that act as cushions. They are located wherever muscles and tendons touch bone. There are over 80 of these sacs on each side of the body. The term "bursitis" is used to describe irritated bursae; this condition can be caused through excessive repetitive movement. It isn't always possible to differentiate inflammation of the overlying tendon from inflamed bursae.

Carpal Tunnel Syndrome

Repetitive motions of fingers, wrists, and arms can cause excessive strain on tendons which can result in swelling. Tendon swelling in the wrist puts pressure on the median nerve lying underneath the wrist tendons, causing Carpal Tunnel Syndrome. (The carpal tunnel is what transmits the flexor tendons and median nerve into the hand.) This syndrome causes pain, tingling, numbness, and/or weakness in the hand and wrist.

When pressure is placed on the median nerve, it will show a measurable loss of conduction. Since the median nerve provides feeling to the front of the thumb, index and middle fingers, and half the ring finger, it is usually quite clear when nerve conduction is being interfered with. Electromyographic testing is used to determine the nerve's condition. Permanent damage may occur if the pressure on the nerve isn't released. Surgery becomes imperative. The transverse carpal ligament is cut to open the tunnel, and then the edges heal together by scar. This scar is unyielding. Occasionally the condition recurs because the scar tissue joins the two edges of the ligament together so tightly that relief isn't obtained until a second operation is conducted.

Disc Injuries

Disc injuries occur when one of the discs between the spinal vertebrae cracks, causing a piece of the hard rim to chip off and lodge itself next to a nerve. Or, the disc's outer hard, fibrous tissue cracks, and the soft inner portion of the disk slowly oozes out.

Hearing Loss

One of the main causes of sound-induced hearing loss is overexposure to excessive sound levels over long periods of time. Musicians exposed to loud percussion or large horn sections on a daily or regular basis without protection (ear plugs or a sound barrier) can develop hearing loss. There are two kinds of hearing loss. One is transient, the other permanent. For instance, after one evening of loud music that literally vibrates your body with sound, you may experience ringing in your ears. Cumulative insults, however, can cause gradual deterioration of the ear drum. These can be caused by a mixture of loud music, daily use of a walkman, a noisy hair dryer or lawn mower, the subway, a band saw, and so on.

Some people will suffer deficits more quickly than others. But once the hearing has been damaged it's for good. Since musicians can't function without their ears, it's important to protect yourself from exposure to equipment or environments that could potentially harm your ear drums. Here are a few suggestions to help avoid deterioration or loss of hearing:

1. Schedule an annual check-up for a base-line hearing test.

2. Be aware of dangerous sound levels.

3. Use devices such as ear plugs or baffles if exposure can't be prevented.

4. If you notice a change in hearing capability, see a specialist immediately .

Hoarseness

This is a condition developed by singers that is usually associated with laryngitis or lesions on the vocal cords. The voice becomes coarse or scratchy. Causes include fatigue, over-singing (too loudly for too long), and improper technique. Healing requires rest and retraining.

Inflammation

Inflammation is the body's local response to cellular injury, characterized by swelling, discoloration, heat, and pain. Through inflammation, the body is increasing the blood flow to an injured area in order to aid in the elimination of harmful toxins and damaged tissue. Rest, ice packs, aspirin, and anti-inflammatory drugs are traditionally used to bring the inflammation down. Drugs should be used as a last resort.

Lactic Acid

The food we eat reaches our muscles in the form of glucose. To create sufficient energy for movement, our muscles burn this glucose. This creates a by-product we call lactic acid. Sustained exercise, including playing a musical instrument, causes lactic acid accumulation at a rate that exceeds the body's ability to excrete it. As lactic acid accumulates, muscle performance is hindered, causing fatigue and undue stress on ligaments, tendons, and bones. Regular rest periods and body work (such as massage or shiatsu) are essential for the elimination of this buildup and the rejuvenation of the muscles.

Muscle Spasms

Muscle spasms are caused by contracting muscle fibers which seize up, bulge, and feel hard to the touch. The resulting symptoms include pain and a tight, tied-up feeling. These spasms are usually triggered by unaccustomed movement or prolonged muscular activity. Massage helps the muscles to release. A hot bath is also helpful.

Muscle Tears

Muscle tears occur when a small cluster of muscle fiber rips or breaks apart. The larger the tear, the more severe the injury. Whether large or small, however, a muscle tear is serious, for when it heals, scar tissue is formed rather than healthy new muscle tissue.

Paresthesias ("Pins and Needles")

Chronic compression of a nerve sends a signal to the brain in the form of a "pins and needles" sensation. This is the body's method of sending a warning signal that something is out of alignment in the spine. Chiropractic adjustment, exercise, and rest are important to help facilitate realignment.

Pinched Nerve

A pinched nerve is a nerve that is being compressed by a protruding piece of a cracked disk or a misplaced vertebra in the neck or spine. This can cause a dull ache in the surrounding area. Generally, massage, rest, or a chiropractic adjustment will alleviate the problem.

Referred Pain

Referred pain is pain felt at a distance from the site of the injury. This phenomenon occurs because sensory nerves travel in pathways.

Sciatica

Sciatica is pain radiating down the legs. It is caused by compression of the large sciatic nerve, which runs down the back of the thigh, or compression of the nerves exiting from the spinal cord that travel to the legs.

Tendinitis

(Tendonitis, Tenosynovitis) Tendons are white, glistening fibrous cords of varied length and thickness that connect muscles to movable structures such as bones. Tendons are housed by thin, filmy tissues called synovial sheaths. The fit should be loose enough to give the tendon room to slide within the sheath. The term "tendinitis" refers to an inflammation of the lining around the tendon due to overuse, or resulting from a tear in the tendon itself between the tendon's attachment to either muscle or bone. Prolonged or abnormal use of the tendon will cause this syndrome, resulting in a tight fit within the sheath and constant pain.

"Tendinitis" is only one of a number of terms describing pain and loss of function associated with excessive activity. The suffix "itis" generally refers to an inflammation present in the tissues, but not all cases of tendinitis have this finding. In addition, specialists in the field often confuse overuse syndromes with tendinitis, and misappropriately treat the condition with corticosteroid injections or anti-inflammatories.

True tendinitis is specific but the inflammation can only be verified by biopsy, which is a surgical procedure used only for research purposes.

Rest — anywhere from one week to three months — will usually work in any event, but if the musician is allowed to continue playing in a tense, contorted, and ultimately dangerous way, the problem will recur. The diagnosis of the underlying cause may therefore be within the realm of the astute music teacher, rather than the doctor.

Remember that tendons take a long time to heal; it's dangerous to stress them prematurely in the healing process because the tendon can tear or re-tear and form scar tissue. After a period of rest and retraining, increase your playing time gradually.

Tennis Elbow

Not just for tennis players, tennis elbow occurs when a tendon near the elbow tears slightly in a "V" shape. Rest is essential in order for healing to take place. You may need to change the way you hold or play your instrument so that injury does not reoccur.

Temporomandibular Joint Dysfunction (TMJ)

The temporomandibular joint is the joint that hinges the lower jaw to the skull. TMJ dysfunctions stem from three primary causes: malocclusion (a problem with the way the upper and lower teeth fit together in an individual's "bite"); habit patterns that place repetitive stress on the lower jaw (grinding of the teeth, chronic tension in the face muscles); and emotional stress, either long or short term. Massage, particularly myotherapy, acupressure and shiatsu, or biofeedback can often take care of TMJ. If the condition is caused by malocclusion, however, professional treatment is mandatory. If long-term emotional stress is the major source factor, psychotherapy would be a useful adjunct to physical therapy.

Trigger Finger

Trigger Finger usually refers to a contraction of the tendon running to the second or third digit through the palm. The result is the permanent flexion of the finger. Surgery is the only cure.

OTHER MUSICAL MATTERS

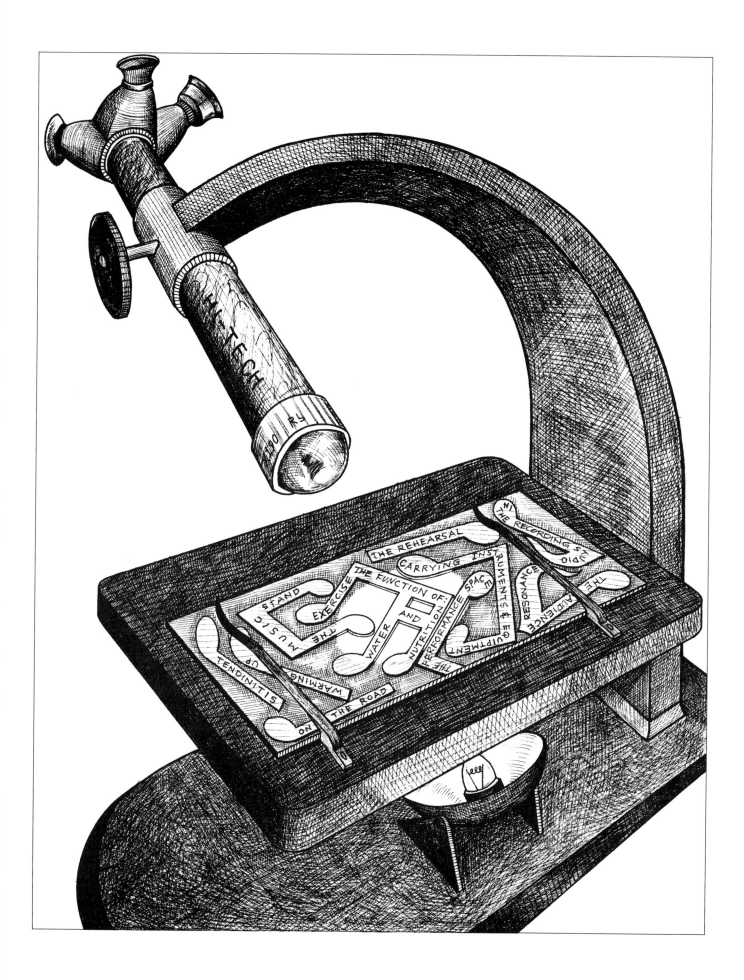

YOU ARE YOUR INSTRUMENT

Nervousness

Nervousness is generally looked upon with dread and as one of the enemies of performance. Many performers fear it so much that they either try to suppress it, which makes it more powerful, or they stop performing altogether.

Nervousness is actually useful and important. It's just that the random side effects can be problematic. These side effects often decrease the level of excellence in performance, but, with adequate preparation, need not be the driving force behind your success or failure on stage.

Reaching one's energies out to a group of people as a performer requires a different physiological "setting" than when you are alone or having an intimate conversation with someone. Your body prepares, and in its infinite wisdom, rearranges internally to free your energies for the performance. If there is food demanding digestive attention, your body will often send it on its way. If you are tired, your blood flow and heart rate will suddenly increase. If you are breathing shallowly or your muscles are tight, you will find yourself yawning.

The Four-Fold Way

1. *Show Up*

2. *Pay Attention: to what is good, true, and beautiful*

3. *Tell the truth without judgement*

4. *Be open to outcome but not attached to outcome*

ANGELES ARRIEN
CROSS-CULTURAL ANTHROPOLOGIST

Shaking, sweating, and tension are all side effects of this energetic shift. Most performers try to get rid of these symptoms. This keeps them focused on what they'd rather forget. When you put a lot of effort into getting rid of certain sensations or feelings, you may actually be helping to keep them in place.

Some performers battle their nerves by repeating to themselves "relax, relax...." This is a verbal instruction to the body. As we've discussed in the units *The Left and Right Hemispheres* and *Sensory Awareness*, verbal instructions are not as effective as imagistic instructions. Creating an actual picture of how you want to feel in your body tends to increase communication with the parasympathetic nervous system, which is in charge of restoration and relaxation.

If you have spent your practice time ignoring your body, the heightening of energy and sensitivity in preparation for performance will feel alien. It may even feel as though your body has been taken over by an outside force — even if this force is, at long last, your life spirit in movement.

If you have trained from a verbal approach, you might suddenly feel "out of control" as the right hemisphere activates and your mode of thinking shifts from exclusive left hemisphere control (sequential memory, and linear, verbal thought) to whole-brain thinking (wholistic, imagistic, and analytical while simultaneously feeling sensation and expressing emotion).

If you have been relying solely on muscle memory to get you through the concert, your hands or mouth may suddenly forget what to do next. The experience of memory loss or a blank mind is appropriate in this situation; you may not have taught your mind the music in the first place! You may not have practiced playing it from auditory memory, from imaging, or from analytical memory. How appropriate that your mind can't help at the very moment that such heightened emotional and sensorial stimuli prevent your hands from operating on automatic!

The control and safety we are accustomed to during practice is threatened by our vulnerability on stage and we tend to keep trying to create security. This is the very moment we need to hear and feel the music; to focus on communicating with the audience; to let go of control and give ourselves over to this incredible experience.

I used to get sick before almost every major performance because I felt so tense, nervous, and afraid. Then one day, I tried consciously opening my heart and loving the audience. From that point on, my health was no longer affected by impending performances. I also discovered that sharing music with other people can be a great deal of fun! The opposite of fear may well be love as far as the physical effect is concerned, because fear promotes restriction, a pulling in, an action of hiding, and love promotes reaching out, an opening of the self to others.

I'm not advocating lying to your audience by trying or pretending to love them when you don't. You can choose to access the essence of love — the openness, vulnerability, and sharing.

As far as I'm concerned, there are four essential ingredients to a successful performance:

- breathe

- suspend time

- have fun

- focus on what you want to accomplish.

Presenting Yourself

How do you feel when someone else is watching you? Do you feel self-conscious? Defensive? Vulnerable? Afraid? Or do you feel at home? Analyze any expectations you have of yourself when in the public eye. Must you act perfectly? Is there some invisible agenda to which you must conform?

Think of situations in which you feel perfectly comfortable. Make a note of that feeling and practice bringing it into your experience when in front of others. Practice

I think it's critical that we begin to dismantle the word "performance" because somehow it implies perfection or some ideal — or doing something for somebody else. When I perform, I don't know how it's going to turn out. And even with a song or a piece of music, I must stay open to the nuances that change it each time and make it present. It's never going to sound like it did yesterday again. Right in that moment you are choosing to engage rather than withdraw. It's profoundly powerful. Technique is — big deal. Beautiful sounds are — big deal. But contact. Real human contact through art, through music, is rare.

SUSAN OSBORN, VOCALIST

allowing yourself to simply be who you are while being watched without trying to hide or change perceived faults and weaknesses. Look into what you need to do to make the performance space your own.

We generally project the issues we have with who we are onto other people when in front of them. They may or may not actually share those issues, but if you truly grant yourself the freedom to be who you are, and your audience the freedom to be who they are, then any concerns you have about what they think and feel becomes a waste of time. Otherwise, your energies will have to go into convincing them that you're worth their time! It's obviously difficult to focus on creating music while grappling with issues of self-worth. Generally, people who are preoccupied with "taking the temperature" of the audience use any negative information — which they obviously just finished inventing — to goose themselves into working harder. While the feelings generated from this activity can produce results (i.e. your playing may very well improve) the quality of experience and relationship to self is degraded.

Even if your audience hates your music, or doesn't think that you are good enough to be on stage — which you could only know if they threw things at you or got up and left — remember that you are there because you love making music enough to devote your life to it.

Performance Preparation

Auralize the piece (hear it in your inner ear), develop an interconnection between muscle memory and your imagistic mind, and learn the internal structure of the piece as well as the names of the notes and chords. If you are a singer, talk through the words, then hum or whistle the melody separately. Instrumentalists, try playing the whole piece with only one hand at a time while imaging and naming the notes.

When you have prepared the music from only one or two parts of the six-fold memory web, mistakes are more likely. If, however, your preparation is complete, there is little chance of memory loss, and the confidence you feel will free you to focus totally on the creation of art.

Beta-Adrenergic Blockers

In many ways, the institution of music — particularly classical — has become a splendid multi-colored bird that has been forced to eat its own tail. The increasing demand for technical perfection and superior playing ability in classical music has fostered a strict selection system of auditions, contests, performances before panels of experts and juries, and competitions against as many as two hundred for a single position in a major symphony orchestra. Jazz, rock, and pop musicians often play for $25 a night in the beginning; if they're among the lucky few, their earnings will jump beyond the imaginable in a game of extreme pressure and high stakes.

The celebrity musician knows that stardom can evaporate at any moment. Minor mistakes can equal disaster and reviews have the power to shape or kill future work. The bird takes another bite of its tail.

Whereas a doctor or lawyer can undergo stressful, exacting training and know that he has a future in his chosen career, the musician has no such certainty. The system has stripped the individual, to a large degree, of personal power.

Given this situation, the beauty of the musical experience has been tainted with fear, jealousy, tremors, shortness of breath, sweaty palms, dryness of mouth, and nausea. The bird takes another bite of its tail...

Thus, the music professor hands the student a miracle drug that will mask or prevent the symptoms of nervousness. The bird takes...

The beta-adrenergic blocking agents were introduced in the sixties. They act as inhibitors of B-adrenoceptors throughout the body, blocking the effects of anxiety, but not the anxiety itself. The theory behind their use is that anxiety feeds upon itself. When an already anxious musician notices that his or her performance is being negatively affected by anxiety, his or her anxiety increases, further affecting the performance, triggering still greater anxiety, and on and on and on. The drug, by blocking tremors, hyperventilation, and tachycardia (rapid heart action) can break the vicious cycle and help the performer gain confidence.

The eight available beta blockers — propranolol, metroprolol, nadolol, atenolol, timolol, pindolol, labetalol, and acebutolol — have a duration of action that extends way beyond the performance. Negative side effects include sleep disturbances, hallucinations, depression, fatigue, and reduction of blood flow to the extremities resulting in cold hands. Beta blockers can also exacerbate allergies, heart failure, and bronchospasm. An increase in triglyceride with a concurrent decrease in high density lipoprotein (HDL) cholesterol levels may occur in some individuals. Generally, a single dose will not produce these effects.

If your performance anxiety is so great that you can't function on stage at all, then using beta-adrenergic blocking agents as part of a stress-management program may be helpful although I do not recommend use of these drugs. In this context, they can be used as a tool to help demonstrate high-level performance, thereby enhancing self-confidence and creating a useful snapshot of a successful performance experience for future reference. Drugs do not address the source of the problem. Make sure that you deal with any emotional/psychological issues instrumental in causing your performance anxiety.

SUGGESTED APPROACH

Be sure to breathe fully and deeply while you do the following techniques.

■ Using the imaging process, see/feel/hear the specifics of how you want your body to function while playing.

■ Create a movie in your mind of your performance — audience, space, music — and image all of the elements and details that you want to have be present.

■ Consciously put the music into all of your memory centers.

Some suggestions about food before performance:

Avoid heavy foods like meat, dairy, and fried food. The digestion of heavy food takes an enormous amount of energy. Your body will be more likely to send heavy foods out the other end right before a performance to lighten up the system and make more energy available for the performance. A heavy meal will also tend to elevate blood sugar levels quickly. Unfortunately, when blood

sugar levels rise too high too fast, they're apt to plummet about 90 minutes later — which would leave you with low energy right in the middle of your performance. Eat lighter foods such as fruit, salad, or vegetables. Complex carbohydrates, such as rice or pasta, won't create a roller-coaster effect with your blood sugar.

Also, drink plenty of water and avoid coffee, tea (unless it's herbal), and caffeinated soft drinks.

Perhaps you can remember a time when you heard a musician who left you untouched emotionally, but had "great technique." The fact of the matter is, that they did not have great technique, because it was overshadowing the meaning of the music. Technique is only as good as it can support, not overshadow, communication.

JEANNIE DEVA, THE CONTEMPORARY VOCALIST

Warming Up

Respect for the warm-up process will give your muscles a longevity and ease that makes listening to your body's needs well worth the time.

There are a number of diverse concepts and styles regarding getting started, ranging from ignoring your body and working it until it does what you want, to dogmatically playing through a series of established warm-up exercises.

The criteria used is generally pro-sound rather than a balance between sound and feeling. There are plenty of wonderful exercises available for warm-up, but if they are utilized from a left-brain orientation, the chances of ascertaining your body's current state and needs — really connecting to how your body is right now — are slim. How your body is right now depends on a variety of factors: diet, rest, amount of misuse or nurturing the day before, emotional state, room temperature, and so on.

When warming up, what you play isn't as important as how you play it.

A left-brain approach entails starting with an intellectual idea of "the proper warm-up exercise" and trying to execute it perfectly while giving mental direction to physical movement. This is quite different than focusing on opening your sensors, reading the current status of your body and mind, asking yourself what you need at that particular moment, and inventing or drawing upon a vocabulary of exercises to tune your muscles, connect with your breath, and activate a clean, clear mind-to-body hook-up.

Warm-up includes sharpening mental focus, establishing the physical and mental settings that will be the most helpful to you while playing, and initiating a fluid oxygen and blood flow through your muscles.

The key to it all is your intention. What physical and mental results do you want to create during warm-up? Intention combined with an accurate reading of your current condition gives important and helpful direction to the body.

Some days you will come to your instrument fluid, connected, and ready to play. Other days you will require a series of specific techniques to reach this state. Learn the difference.

When you turn on a computer, in addition to the required electricity (food, oxygen, and blood circulating through the body) the computer requires a program to

If you elongate your muscles slowly and regularly they will remain elongated for longer and longer periods of time. Few people have the patience to do this and instead force their muscles to get a quick result. When you force muscles to stretch they spring back to a tight position and often damage muscle or tendon tissue.

DR. BEN E. BENJAMIN, LISTEN TO YOUR PAIN

be able to perform the desired functions. Whether you want to breathe freely while playing, be posturally aligned, play with a relaxed thumb, or be connected emotionally, these elements of your music-making stand a much greater chance of being present if you program them in during your warm-up. And if you use the warm-up period to listen to your body and establish your goals, you'll be well on your way to a productive and satisfying session.

In addition, it literally does take from .5 to 2 minutes for the actual muscle tissue to warm up and it's useful to understand the process that takes place.

All cells in the body require fuel for energy (*adrenosine triphosphate* or *ATP*). Five to six seconds worth of ATP is stored in each cell. If you keep moving, the body will use stores *of* creatine phosphate, and convert it into ATP as is needed, but there's only enough for an additional 20 - 25 seconds of intense activity. This means that if you jump into a great deal of frenetic activity immediately, your body will use a process called *anaerobic metabolism* and, after 30 seconds, revert to burning glu-

cose to produce energy. For each ATP formed out of each glucose (2 to 1), a lactic acid is also formed. Energy production via this pathway is limited by this accumulation of lactic acid, because lactic acid produces fatigue.

The more desirable process, which is called *aerobic metabolism* or *oxidative phosphorylation*, utilizes fats as well as glucose and glycogen to create ATP. This form of metabolism is fairly slow and can provide energy for almost unlimited duration. Typically, it takes about .5 to 2 minutes for aerobic metabolism to adjust to the increased demands of exercise — if you are moving with a slow, consistent rhythm. When this mechanism kicks in, we experience something we refer to as second wind.

When we combine this information with the fact that if you stretch a muscle too quickly or use it in ways it's not ready for, it will contract vigorously to protect itself, there is enough evidence pointing out the importance of beginning every practice session with slow, gentle activity.

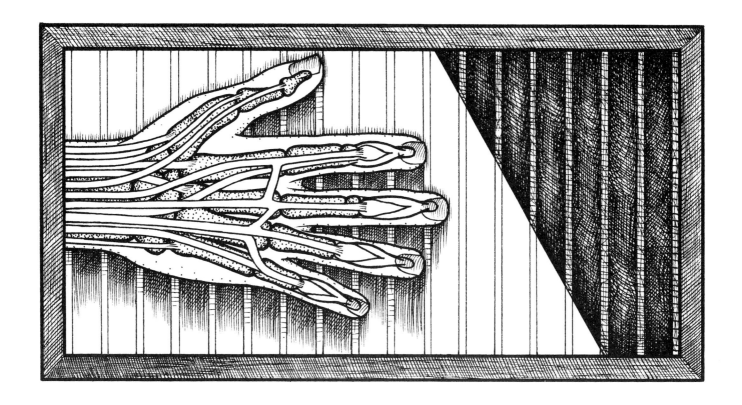

The Music Lesson

"This is the one hour when I can really be myself and do what I love most!" I think that this is the highest compliment a teacher can receive from a student. Yet so often, students feel the opposite in anticipation of their lesson. I maintain that health includes one's physical and mental states. I've seen and experienced some extremely healthy teacher-students relationships; I've also seen great harm occur within the work process — sometimes without total recovery on the part of the student.

The relationship between student and teacher is a fascinating and complex one. While students may think that they are just going to an expert to learn how to place their hands or lips in the right place at the right time, so much more takes place within that weekly hour. Their relationship to the teacher often reflects their response to and interaction with authority. The work process reflects how they typically go about creating what they want (the good and the bad), as well as how they deal with their expectations of themselves. The learning skills they have mastered or haphazardly collected will be the only means through which they can obtain information from their teacher, unless those skills are addressed and developed within the lesson. Choosing the best teacher to work with can have an enormous impact on your physical and mental health as a musician.

Similarly, the teacher brings much more than instrumental expertise to the work process. Life philosophy, level of self-realization, weaknesses, fears, relationship needs, and parental philosophy (whether or not the individual actually has children of his or her own) can, and do often enter into the work process.

I've heard stories of teachers who verbally strike or punish their students to discipline them. I've also heard stories of teachers who've helped their students access tremendous growth and healing, becoming the most inspiring force in the student's entire life.

Just as trust and communication are essential to the success of this working relationship, independent thinking is equally important. If you have been raised to think that complete trust means that you should stop thinking for yourself and turn yourself over to your teacher, you are actually endangering yourself in at least two ways: you are opening yourself up to potential hurt from their undeveloped side, and you are not learning how to build your own power, something that is essential to successful music-making.

There are two basic methods of teaching. The teacher can employ the "monkey-see, monkey-do" method. Here the students simply imitate the teacher without any analysis or understanding of why a particular thing must be done a particular way beyond the fact that "an expert" said so! Or, the teacher can teach the principle behind each aspect of the theme being discussed or worked on. This enables the students to develop the ability to think for themselves and to apply these principles in an accelerated fashion on their own, automatically developing their technique on a consistent basis rather than waiting to be spoon-fed the next morsel of information.

How your teacher interacts with you while you are learning is of essential importance, because his or her voice tends to become internalized. If you have internalized a harsh, reprimanding, controlling voice, you will jump on yourself for every little mistake, and tend to feel that you are not, in fact, in control of what you do. It will almost seem as though luck gets you through the correct moves. I consider this a very nonintegrated, nonmusical experience. If your teacher's instructional methods embody support, encouragement, respect for your ability to reason, and respect for your freedom as an individual, you will automatically internalize these qualities; they will become the foundation of your technique. You will tend to develop an inner voice that coaches you to play well; it will be a friendly and supportive voice.

Technique has been traditionally defined as being about mastering the micro-movements necessary to command a musical instrument. But technique includes so much more. It can actually include how you use your mind and body to interact, learn, practice, and perform.

SUGGESTED APPROACH

Take some time to analyze and write down your tendencies in each of the following areas:

Authority

Notice how you tend to interact with authority figures in your life. Do you automatically rebel? Do you turn to them for leadership? Do you interact the same way with them as with other people with whom you have close work and personal relationships? Take some time to think this through; make a conscious choice about what kind of relationship you wish to have with the experts you turn to for information.

Learning Habits and Skills

How do you learn? Do you best assimilate information through verbal directions, physical demonstration, the use of metaphors, mental pictures, and stories — or a combination of all three? If your teacher does not speak your language, you may think that there is something wrong with you when you learn slowly, yet it may just be a communication problem. Take note of the subjects you tend to learn quickly and easily. Try to analyze the nature of these subjects as well as the learning process. If you are a circle, don't try to squeeze yourself into a square: if your teacher can't adapt to your language of learning, find a teacher who can.

Momentum

What types of actions do you take when you want something? Do you procrastinate before becoming involved? Do you leap in and then peter out? Do you make a decision, take action consistently, and then change over to a totally different project just before completion? Do you take a lot of action with an expectation about when and what kind of results you should get, become frustrated if the results don't fit the ideal, and then give up?

Stop and analyze your typical pattern. Knowledge can mean recognition in the middle of the cycle, thereby enabling you to make more informed decisions mid-process. Remember that results grow out of a build in momentum. Momentum is created by consistent action, no matter what.

Principles

Teach yourself the difference between principles and rules by practicing converting one to the other. Here are some examples:

- *Rule:* Always place your thumb... (in such and such a position)

- *Principle:* Paying attention to the anatomy of the hand fosters healthy muscle use.

- *Rule*: Never trust a new teacher.

- *Principle:* It's easier to predict the behavior of someone whose actions are familiar to you.

- *Rule:* Always warm up before playing difficult musical pieces.

- *Principle*: Muscles tend to respond more efficiently when they receive focussed information from the mind, and when the circulation of blood — and therefore warmth — is increased.

Expectations

Choosing what you want to create and then using the best actions you can think of to realize your vision is very different from expecting something of yourself and then punishing yourself when you don't live up to that expectation. Often expectations are designed to raise internal conflict sufficient to inspire action toward a goal. The internal war becomes a pressure cooker that eventually leads to action. The problem with this method of creating is that the individual is engaging in a kind of self-manipulation. This method of self-interaction fosters a lousy quality of experience along the way, and can break down the moment you allow yourself to feel better. Since conflict was generating action, if the conflict is lessened or removed, so is the action.

Practice taking action purely because you choose to and for no other reason than to support creating what you want.

Read "The Path of Least Resistance" by Robert Fritz.

Tempo, Tempo

In my folk festival days, I remember a fiddler popping up on the scene who wowed the audience with his lightening-fast solos. He was fifteen years old and I felt extremely jealous of him because I was seven years his senior and couldn't play as fast. Within two years, he had to have surgery on both of his wrists. I haven't heard his name mentioned since, but I did learn that all too often we mistakenly think of playing fast as the ultimate goal. In the push for speed, we forget to hear the music, to breathe, or to create physical movement that is fluid. By equating speed with mastery, we tend to mute our ability to make and monitor healthy priorities.

Time is defined by our subjective experience. We could even go so far as to say that time does not exist, that the flow of linear time is a totally psychological event. Yes, there are specific metronome settings for specific pieces of music, but I'm talking about what happens when effort becomes confused with accomplishment. I call this the *false feedback phenomena*: the musician is using a certain type of physical sensation as a standard of measurement. In this case, the effort expended to play fast has been incorrectly linked with mastery or success. *Effort* is not what it takes to play fast. It takes supreme *relaxation*. Playing slowly actually requires more effort and control.

Many musicians are aware that relaxation, as well as attention to quality of sound and experience are prerequisites to an increase in speed. In some situations, like at a group jam session, a private lesson, or a performance, it can be quite challenging to stay aligned with one's priorities. In fact, many of my students complain that in group situations everyone tends to play too fast, that they have no control over this, and are forced to strain. Often some combination of nervousness, excitement and competition is a dominant factor in these situations.

I've found that fear seems to trigger a control response in which the left brain tends to take over; almost everyone resorts to thinking the notes in a linear fashion rather than hearing and feeling the music.

It's essential to learn how to speak up in group situations. You will be surprised to find that many of your fellow musicians will be relieved that someone has taken charge and helped to facilitate a relaxed environment. But, if you initiate a change and the group isn't responsive, maybe these aren't the people to be jamming with!

I've found that stopping to take a few slow, deep breaths while under stress can make an immediate difference. The pause before beginning signifies that you are taking charge of the performance space. The audience (or teacher) will naturally breathe with you. A process called "entrainment" occurs. This is when one individual establishes a rhythmic relationship with another. Just as it can take place between the listener and the musician, entrainment can occur between a mother and her baby, or even between an individual and nature.

Music exists as a flow of sound that has its own integrity, its own heartbeat. Finding that heartbeat from a muscularly fluid, musically in-tune orientation can yield a totally different experience and sound. The change in orientation can be engaged when you take control and focus on listening, breathing, and feeling.

SUGGESTED APPROACH

Start an exercise or piece of music with the metronome set at 40. Use the following questions to determine when to move the tempo up to the next notch, and then the next:

- Are my muscles straining to accomplish this or are they relaxed?

- Am I breathing?

- Is my tone resonant and full, but not forced?

- Are my pitches accurate?

- Am I using my ability to hear the music in my inner ear to generate sound?

- Do I know where I am and what I'm doing at all times?

- If I put my instrument down, would I be able to image playing at this speed? (See *Visualization and The Imagistic Mind*)

The Ensemble

Group energy is a fascinating phenomenon. It can be a vehicle for co-creation, sharing and joy; it can also take on a life of its own, pushing the individual into unpleasant, dangerous, and atypical behavior.

Some musicians think that playing with other people involves repeating what you practiced alone in a group setting. Others step into the group with such a concern for measuring up that they willingly bend themselves out of shape for the sake of looking good and gaining acceptance. Both approaches are bound to contribute to misery and injury.

Playing faster than you are ready to and playing louder than necessary generally invites trouble. Yet many players willingly plow on, thinking they're the only one who is feeling strained.

Putting aside a quality experience and making yourself vulnerable to injury can hardly be justified by a concern for high ratings. Yet, many players opt for this trade-off. I know a musician who ignored her body's signals in an effort to live up to the speed and hot licks her group required and eventually had to stop playing for several years!

Listen to your colleagues; communicate your needs and respect the needs of the other players. The ensemble experience can be an incredibly inspiring, rich exchange with other musicians.

The Rehearsal

The rehearsal is a warm-up. It's an opportunity to learn how to listen to one another, to build trust and a common language, and to experiment before making final decisions and agreements. The rehearsal is not about arriving at a final product right away; that doesn't happen until right before the performance.

If you are uncomfortable in any way, the rehearsal is the time to speak up and make adjustments. And this is the time to learn about your fellow musicians' needs. If you intimidate or ignore your colleagues, they won't do their best playing. If you allow someone to intimidate you, the same can occur.

Note: Professional players often find themselves in on-demand sessions where there is no opportunity to warm up and individual need is secondary to churning out the product. There is a greater taboo for speaking up in these situations and those that do are often considered troublemakers, even by their fellow musicians. Yet, when you do have the courage to speak out, everyone benefits. Don't mistake being professional for turning into a machine or being an "excellent shoemaker." The producer may be willing to accept mechanically perfect music; are you willing to create it? And, more importantly, are you willing to treat your body that way?

YOU ARE YOUR INSTRUMENT

Sight-Reading Music

We are a very visual society. Studies have shown that when we use our eyes, we tend to shut down our other senses approximately 80%! When we read music, we are translating symbols into micro-movements. Instruction in sight-reading generally focuses on seeing a note, knowing its name, and assigning it a place on the instrument. While ear-training then assigns pitch to the symbols, that usually comes later and only if the student attends ear-training classes.

Often musicians do not hear the music when they look at the sheet music. They use the symbols to tell them what notes to play, and hear the music only after playing the notes. Even then, their attention is on translating the next series of written symbols into finger placement.

When I ask a student to whistle or sing the piece they've just read, they often have little or no auditory memory of it! This is ironic. The love and excitement we feel about music that inspires us to master an instrument has not been connected to how most of us spend 90% of our time learning it!

As discussed in the unit *Six-Fold Memory*, auditory memory is essential to learning music. Waiting until one's fingers can play the notes perfectly before learning the music is taking a backwards, misguided approach. In addition, it's a mechanical approach that is not only time-consuming but deadening to one's sensory awareness. It's all too easy to ignore one's posture, breath, and physical relationship to the instrument when one is visually focused on the sheet music.

SUGGESTED APPROACH

■ Practice reading through a piece of music without your instrument. Try to hear first the rhythms, and then the pitches in your inner ear. This might be a slow process for you at first, but as you repeat it, you will develop greater and greater facility with it.

■ Play a measure, turn away from the music stand, and sing or whistle what you've just played. Then play it from memory, even if you have to slip and slide a little.

■ Find a friend who is willing to play a call-and-response game with you; he or she plays the music to you in short phrases and you play it back. Gradually lengthen the phrases to improve auditory memory.

■ Tape yourself playing a piece from sheet music. Then learn the music by playing along with the tape.

In the Recording Studio

The demands of taping note-perfect music in a finite amount of time in a recording studio often obscure a quality experience. The long, yet paradoxically limited, hours require perfection again and again. If you don't see to it that you play with relaxed and fluid muscles, stamina diminishes and it becomes increasingly more difficult to play well.

Approach a stint in the recording studio the way an athlete approaches the Olympics. In addition to developing a whole-brain relationship to music-making that includes sensory awareness, muscular fluidity, and six-fold memory, it's essential to build your stamina in preparation. If you tend to practice one to three hours a day, but plan to be in the recording studio seven hours a day, you are going to create physical problems unless you build up your practice time incrementally, using muscle balance and healing techniques to keep your body healthy and tension-free.

Improvising cellist David Darling describes going into such painful muscle spasms after completing his first ECM recording in 1981 that he had to de-board his plane before it left Germany for home.

After three days of playing seven hours a day, his left hand began to cramp so badly that he started to hyperventillate. Though his breathing mechanism had been triggered by fear, he didn't know that, and thought he was having a heart attack. He was rushed to the hospital.

When David returned home, his doctor prescribed a muscle relaxant. He did not mention to David the need to make a change in his technique nor did he recommend physical therapy. Never having had a problem like this before, and assuming his doctor knew best, David took the prescribed medication. While we know a great deal about the dangers of valium and zanax now, thanks to the plethora of newspaper articles relating horror stories, this information was not common knowledge in 1981.

As is often the case in a situation like this, the psychological scars were more difficult to live with than the actual physical problem. Every concert was shadowed by the fear of a reoccurence. This, in addition to the addictive nature of the drug, placed David in a fragile situation; he was afraid that if he stopped taking the drug, he would not be able to function professionally.

He finally had to endure the physical and mental process of withdrawal on his own. Afterwards, because he was fortunate enough to be a part of the New Age community, many healers helped him learn how to breathe properly as well as how to release and use his muscles properly.

In addition to a careful preparation for the recording session, there are some specific guidelines you can follow while in the studio that will allow you to avoid such a dramatic episode, and actually help you create a quality recording experience.

■ Establish a rapport with the engineer. His or her understanding of your needs can affect your ability to create the sound you want. Even though the music is recorded flat first and equalized during the mix, you must be satisfied with the sound you hear or you'll inadvertently push to compensate. Make sure that you are happy with the headphone or playback speaker equalization and that you can hear a good balance of all the instruments.

■ Warm up your lungs and your muscles by stretching, moving, and doing some conscious deep breathing when you first arrive. Take breaks to stretch and shake out. (See GLOSSARY for recommended techniques.)

■ Drink lots of water.

■ Avoid caffeine, chocolate, and other stimulants. After the initial rush, they can interfere with muscle coordination. Remember that your muscles need nutrition, not artificial stimulation.

■ Don't eat heavy, rich foods or large meals before or during a session. Your system will be so busy with digestion that you'll tend to feel heavy and sluggish.

■ If you feel yourself pushing or straining, lighten up or stop. (See *Natural Biofeedback* unit). Use images to aid your muscles: turn your arms into rubber, become a flowing river, or use whatever image seems intuitively right. (See *Sensory Awareness* unit.)

■ Stay warm. Always bring extra layers. Some studios aren't well heated and others blast air conditioning (even in the winter) to cool off the machines.

■ Remember the key: do whatever you need to do to feel comfortable before and during the session.

Environmental Hazards

There are certain environmental hazards of which we must be aware and, whenever possible, avoid.

Outdoor concerts in the sun, bug spray, toxic chemicals, and cigarette smoke pose the greatest health threats. Sometimes one person can create change by educating others and voicing concern. The more we musicians speak up, the greater the impact!

Outdoor Concerts

Outdoor concerts in the noon-day sun may seem like a lovely idea to the producer, but are quite injurious to the performer's energies, skin, and instrument. When booked for an outdoor concert, always insist that protection from the sun be included in the contract. That protection could range from a simple tree to an umbrella or band shell. Also make sure that you're supplied with plenty of water.

Another hazard of outdoor concerts, particularly those held in the evening, is that bug spray is often used to reduce the number of mosquitoes and moths, many times right before the concert. These sprays are mildly irritating to the unsuspecting audience member, but if the engagement is an ongoing one, the real threat is to the musician, who must inhale the poisonous fumes night after night.

Find out what they are spraying, how often, and where. Some bug sprays are less toxic than others. Take an active role in voicing your opinion as your conscience and concerns dictate.

Toxic Chemicals

Musicians who perform for theater and dance concerts are exposed to toxic chemicals during rehearsal, often without even realizing it! Spray paint, glue, and any other number of pollutants are used to build and decorate the set. Ask that the activities that fill the space with dust or chemicals be done when you aren't present and that proper ventilation be used.

Cigarette Smoke

Even if you yourself smoke, nightly exposure to massive amounts of smoke in clubs contributes to lung cancer and denies your body the proper amount of oxygen it needs to feed your muscles as you use them. You can ask that smoking be banned or limited, or that proper ventilation be provided.

The Function of Exercise, Nutrition, and Water

There are numerous books that deal specifically with nutrition and exercise. Because it is so essential for the musician to stay in peak playing (and living) condition, these subjects bear your attention. The following is simply a synopsis of some of the key elements.

Water

Our bodies are composed of 70% water. Water acts as a solvent in the body, carrying toxins out of the cells, and nutrients in. Since the digestive system regards juice, soda, and coffee as food (not water), it's important to cellular functions for our bodies to receive adequate water in its pure state. Six to eight glasses a day are recommended.

Just as you wouldn't hesitate to supply your car with gas on a regular basis, "water your body"!

Nutrition

Our muscles also require a specific balance of many nutrients for optimum function. Calcium, in particular, is important to the muscles as it helps prevent cramping. Make sure that your diet is well balanced and that it includes more whole foods than processed. Fresh food is always the richest in nutrition and frozen food is usually better than canned.

A well balanced diet consists of proteins, grains, fruit, and vegetables. Tissue irritants and food with no nutritive value should be avoided. These include sugar, caffeine, chocolate, and soda.*

Drugs, cigarettes, and alcohol take an even heavier toll on the body. Remember that what you put in today will be what you'll have to work with tomorrow.

Exercise

As we've discussed earlier in the book, our muscles are incredibly receptive to whatever input we offer them — whether that input is haphazard or conscious. Repetitive motion will tend to overuse certain muscle groups while not calling upon others. It's essential to our overall health to keep all of our muscles toned and balanced. Otherwise, the skeleton can become misaligned, causing various kinds of health problems. In addition, exercise increases circulation, assisting in the elimination of various toxins (lactic acid, fat, chemical residue, and so on) from the muscles. And finally, exercise increases your energy level and your physical stamina. If you think you're too tired to exercise, it's a sure bet you're not exercising enough!

Try exercising three times a week for just a few weeks. You're likely to discover that you sleep better at night and feel more alert during the day. The better you feel, the better you will play.

*Note: Singers should be wary of dairy products as they tend to be mucous-producing. While some feel the congestive effects of dairy products, others do not. Experiment and see what effect, if any, they have on you.

Carrying Instruments and Heavy Equipment

Since going to a rehearsal or performance nowadays often means carrying more than just an instrument, there are additional physical challenges with which you must contend.

How often musicians say, "By the time I got to the gig I was so tired from carrying everything that I didn't have enough energy to play." Amps, electronic effects, electric instruments, set decorations, and luggage take their toll on our backs, hands, and fingers. While hiring a roady is probably the best solution, we don't always have money in the budget to cover such luxuries.

The following can be used to help this situation:

Knapsack: Heavy shoulder-bags cut into the shoulders; a knapsack distributes the weight evenly across your back and shoulders.

Luggage Cart: A cart, particularly one that is collapsible and has wheels, can reduce your load by 100%. They fold up for storage and are easy to navigate over curbs. Ask someone to grab the bottom when going up stairs.

Lifting: Bend your knees when you lift heavy objects and stay close to your center of gravity. Accustom yourself to the feeling of lifting from your legs, not your back. Do this by consciously trying to absorb the weight into your thighs. Breathe deeply, exhaling during the lift. If you feel pain in your back when lifting STOP and get someone to help you.

YOU ARE YOUR INSTRUMENT

On The Road

Touring presents a whole new series of physical challenges: carrying luggage; sitting for long periods of time; dietary changes; shifts in the time zone; sharp environmental shifts, such as swings from humid to dry, hot to cold; unfamiliar pillows and beds and the resulting fitful sleep; and all the tension that can come from adapting to new people, environments, and technical snafus.

Here are some simple suggestions that can aid you in your travels.

Musician's Travel Kit:

tiger balm (and an old t-shirt or bandana)

bath salts

scarf

jacket

magic wand massage vibrator

SUGGESTED APPROACH

While traveling, carry oil and/or tiger's balm to massage your muscles. The balm will heat up the area it permeates. A massage wand will also help jiggle out the tension. Take a hot bath at the end of a long day. Keep your body warm. Remember that every space has a different thermostat aesthetic! Drink at least six glasses of water a day, particularly while flying; be careful not to drink alcohol while on an airplane. Keep your neck and body warm at all times, and counteract any long periods spent sitting with simple physical movements (swing your arms or legs, stretch, and so on depending upon space allowance). A twenty minute walk while swinging your arms and breathing deeply is an excellent re-charger. You can also use *Pendulum Swings*, *Hula Hoops* (See GLOSSARY), *Yoga*, and any other gentle exercises to encourage circulation.

The Performance Space

Each performance space is unique, placing different demands on the performer. The acoustics vary; the audience can seem like they're a mile away or right on top of the stage; the ensemble's spatial arrangement can change; the amplification equipment for jazz and rock musicians can range from lousy to excellent, sometimes lacking a monitor speaker or proper equalization. Everything that was practiced so successfully at home in familiar territory now sounds alien and new.

Often we arrive with a fixed idea of the ideal conditions we need in order to play well. Our expectations are rarely met unless we've achieved the status that few musicians are granted in a country where artists are generally not considered important unless famous in the media. It's important to let go of these expectations.

Learn how to tune your ears to various settings and practice "simultaneous listening." This is the ability to hear in your "inner ear" the sound you are creating, as well as the music of the rest of the ensemble, the music as it moves out into the space, and the music of your imagination (if you're improvising) — all simultaneously! Your listening mechanism becomes a bit like a mixer in that it has the ability to hear it all in balance.

SUGGESTED APPROACH

Get as much information as you can before you arrive. Compile a list of questions that you automatically ask each time so that nothing is left out:

- Seating capacity

- Equipment (number of mikes, monitor, stands, chairs, staff help, type of mixing board, etc.)

- Spatial set-up

- Amount of time for sound check (can you come in a day or so before the concert to warm up in the space?)

- Size of stage

- Heating/air-conditioning

- Carpet or wood floor

Take some time to get to know the space. Walk around; familiarize yourself with the acoustics; stand center stage and imagine how the space will feel when filled with audience. Find a way to make the space your own.

If, after all of this preparation, you begin the concert and aren't satisfied, between pieces change whatever you need to change in order to be comfortable. The audience will understand. Include them in the process. It can be a wonderful way of establishing a closer relationship. You can even create humor in the situation.

Give yourself permission to move while playing. There's nothing wrong with changing position, carrying something somewhere in the middle of singing or playing, signaling the sound person, and so on. Actively create what you need to make the space your own.

The Audience Resonance

One afternoon while listening to a friend's vocal recital, I noticed that one of my shoulders was hurting me. On closer inspection, I realized that I had been holding it in a raised position for quite some time, which was highly unusual for me.

I looked around and noticed that the man directly in front of me was sitting with his shoulder raised, as was the woman in front of him. I then noticed that my friend had been resting one arm on the piano while singing. She had forgotten about it and had gradually raised her shoulder.

The audience arrives ready to receive. Even those whose minds chatter on and on, critiquing, analyzing, and assessing, are more receptive than they realize. It is rather difficult to receive selectively. All that takes place on stage, whether conscious or unconscious, is beamed out as if the performer were a transmitter, and the audience, the receiver.

I am convinced that the way we receive music opens a kind of psychic resonance. In a series of experiments with my students, we've played with this phenomena. The performing student would visualize a landscape, a specific color or a specific smell, and play for us while focusing on it. After listening to the music, we'd each describe what we saw/felt/tasted with roughly 80% accuracy.

In other words, if while playing, the student focused on tasting lemon, most of us would taste lemon or something tart and tangy while listening.

Imagine what you give your audience when holding your breath, thinking about technique, fearing mistakes, or worrying about how you're doing! Relating to the audience consciously, whether or not you agree that the performer can determine relationship and input, gives you a performance orientation that is much more powerful and full of exciting possibilities.

While you can't manipulate or control how your audience interacts with you, you can determine your own experience on stage as well as what you make available to your listeners. Some ways of thinking about things are more powerful than others. Experiment.

SUGGESTED APPROACH

Imagine that the audience says yes to everything you send them. If you think of them as critical, they say yes and watch you critically. If you think of them as being distant, they say yes and remain aloof.

Experiment with seeing/feeling the qualities and relationship you want to experience on stage and in the music. What do you want to communicate? Where do you want to take your listeners? Where do you want to travel as you perform? Hold these images as a vision in preparation for and during the concert.

YOU ARE YOUR INSTRUMENT

The Musician As Dancer

In the science of healing, there are plenty of talented and valuable medical consultants, but it is the responsibility of the individual to be the ultimate expert about his or her own body. No one else can tell us exactly what and how much we feel something; this is a job each of us must do on our own. What we learn, largely through trial and error, may apply to others, but it applies most specifically to ourselves. Drugs and Ace bandages cannot possible increase our mastery over the intricate way we "wear our bodies" while playing. Nor can they teach us the root cause of the very technical dysfunctions that engender soreness or injury. A doctor cannot help us to sensitize ourselves to ourselves.

While medical experts are important resources to us, they seek cures that will work for everybody; we seek fine-tuned individual solutions through the expansion of intimate first-hand knowledge of our own bodies. Conscious experimentation and observation become our most important tools for determining the most effective means of creating and sustaining health.

Our structure-seeking tendency and our constant effort toward mastery tends to promote searching for the "one right way" and staying there. Mastering our instrument while simultaneously increasing our health requires flexibility of mind and body, much in the spirit of the tight-rope walker or dancer.

Like dancers, we, too are constantly juggling with balance, contraction and release, fluidity of movement, precision, and expression. In our journey toward mastery of the creation of music, we reflect, embody and express the dance of life

Where is the music? You can find it at many levels — in the vibrating strings, the trip of the hammers, the fingers striking the keys, the black marks on the paper, or the nerve impulses produced in the player's brain. But all of these are just codes; the reality of music is the shimmering, beautiful, invisible form that haunts our memories without ever being present in the physical world.

DEEPAK CHOPRA, QUANTUM HEALING

YOU ARE YOUR INSTRUMENT

Muscle Balance Glossary

Muscle Balance Glossary

The following section contains all of the muscle balance techniques and approaches to healing and relaxation mentioned in each of the previous units on the body. They are useful for prevention of injury, maintenance of health, and after-the-fact healing. Almost any form of exercise can help rejuvenate and balance the muscles as long as you are sensitive to your body's needs, breathe deeply while moving, and know when to stop.

ARM LIFTS I

← Lie on your stomach with your forehead touching the floor, chin tucked slightly under and your arms resting straight out in front of you. As you exhale, lift arms straight up off the floor. Hold for 3 - 5 seconds; as you inhale, move your arms slowly back down into a rest position. Repeat 10 - 30 times.

This movement strengthens the upper back and helps balance the body after activity that has focused the body forward for a long period of time.

ARM LIFTS II

→ Now bend your arms before lifting, palms facing the floor. These lifts focus on a slightly different muscle group. Both approaches are helpful for strengthening the upper back muscles.

ARM SHAKES

Keeping your arms slightly bent at the elbows, shake them gently for several minutes until flesh and muscle soften and "loosen" from bone. You should feel a tingling sensation afterwards.

This movement helps release tension. It also teaches you how to give your arm weight to gravity. You can then re-create this relaxation while playing.

CONSTRUCTIVE REST

There are times when even the most careful and conscious musician's body has reached its physical limit. In this case, there is nothing more healing than a day or two, or even a week, of total rest or relaxing activity. You will usually notice that when you return to playing you've improved; you've most likely assimilated many of the techniques and concepts you were working on prior to your rest, and simultaneously rejuvenated your muscle tissue.

To weave this rejuvenation cycle into your actual practice time, separate your time into short segments sandwiched by body work, imaging and rest. Use the *Constructive Rest Position.*

CONSTRUCTIVE REST POSITION

Lie down on your back on the floor, with a book under your head or a rolled towel under your neck. Bend your knees or rest your calves on a bench or chair. Breathe deeply and release your body weight into the floor. The small of your back should easily touch the floor in this position. (You can use this time to "free-float" or to image playing.)

The Constructive Rest Position gives your spine an opportunity to align and your muscles to relax. Your bent knees will be a relief to the small of your back, particularly if you have been standing while playing. Five to twenty minutes can work wonders in this position. Afterwards, stand up by first rolling onto your side; then come up onto your knees or into a seated position.

FREEDOM AXIS

To determine the best position for your arms if you play an instrument that requires a lifted position, such as the violin or viola, place your elbow by your side with your arm bent. Lift without raising your shoulder. You should notice that distance is limited; in order to lift completely, you would have to raise your shoulder as well.

Since playing in this position will strain the shoulder, back, and neck and mobility will be greatly hampered, it is not recommended.

Now repeat this motion with your elbow starting over your hip bone, which will require you to move your arm in front of your body. You'll discover greater mobility from this forward arm placement. In fact, you should be able to lift your elbow above your head without straining or lifting your shoulder.

Hang Over

Stand with your knees slightly bent and your feet aligned under your hips. Tuck your chin to your chest and slowly bend over, imagining that you are releasing your spine forward vertebra by vertebra. If your hands and forearms can touch the floor, great. If not, just go as far toward the floor as you comfortably can.

Make sure you keep your head and neck relaxed and your knees slightly bent. After "hanging out" in this position for a few minutes, gently bend and straighten your knees several times; make sure you don't lock them. Then straighten back up to standing very slowly, again using the image of moving vertebra by vertebra. Bring your head up last.

When standing for long periods of time, the lower back and leg muscles tend to shorten, particularly when the arms are raised; this technique helps lengthen and relax those muscles.

HEAD LIFTS

On all fours, supporting your weight with your hands and knees, relax your neck muscles completely and allow your head to hang loosely. Then, as you inhale, slowly lift it all the way up, and just as slowly lower it to the starting position on an exhale. Repeat this 10 - 30 times.

These movements increase strength in the neck and help hold the vertebrae in alignment. They also give the neck muscles an opportunity to be stretched, balancing the tendency to hold the neck in one fixed position while playing or singing.

Also lift your head up to the right 10 - 30 times and then to the left. This is done without turning the head; simply lift it using the neck muscles.

HOT AND COLD

Temperature can be used to affect the muscles. When there is extreme swelling from injury or tendinitis, use ice or cold water to bring the swelling down. For soreness or stiffness, a hot bath or heat can be used to relax the muscles. Moist heat is superior to dry heat. Current medical opinion suggests alternating hot and cold for most muscular injuries. (Do this for roughly 15 to 30 minutes at a time.) While using heat or cold, it's important to remember to keep moving one's body when injured to promote circulation and to keep the new-forming tissue pliable and healthy.

Heat

A particularly powerful use of heat for muscle release and rejuvenation is the Edgar Cayce Castor Oil Pack.* Buy pure castor oil and unbleached flannel from your local health food store. Soak the flannel in some castor oil and place it on the area that has been overworked. (The flannel should not be so wet that it is dripping.)

Place a piece of plastic over the flannel, a towel over the plastic and a heating pad over the towel. Rest comfortably for an hour, varying the level of heat every five to ten minutes. Rinse the castor oil off with water mixed with baking soda. Repeat every other night for a total of three sessions. You should feel a huge difference.

Cold

Dr. Ben E. Benjamin, author of "Listen to Your Pain," prescribes ice treatment to his patients as a tool for healing muscle injury. He notes that ice numbs the pain so the injured area can be moved, rather than held in a protective but stifling manner. This permits the body to heal more quickly.

After chilling the area for five to twenty minutes, begin to move it slowly and gently, gradually increasing the range of motion. When the numbness wears off, reapply the ice. Repeat this cycle a number of times (or as long as you can stand it!)

*Note: Castor oil is very difficult to get out of sheets and clothing so be careful to use an old towel and to protect your linens. Use a fresh piece of flannel every few sessions.

Hula Hoops

Stand with your knees slightly bent and your feet aligned under your hips. Slowly rotate your hips, first clockwise for a minute, then counterclockwise, as if you were twirling a hula hoop in slow motion. Keep your body and arms relaxed.

This movement relaxes and lengthens your lower back muscles as well as the muscles in your sides and hip joints. It also warms up the spine and trains your torso to be agile rather than static.

Imaging

During the healing process, taking a break from playing is essential. It gives one's muscles an opportunity to rest and rejuvenate. The old patterns stored in muscle memory begin to fade, creating greater opportunity for re-education.

You can continue to improve technically and learn new music during the healing process by practicing in your mind. As we discussed in *Visualization and the Imagistic Mind*, imaging accesses the right hemisphere and enables you to see/feel/hear the "whole picture." Since our bodies respond to mental direction, imaging creates a strong foundation for establishing new muscular/technical patterns.

In addition to using imaging as a tool for improvement during the healing process, you can use a few minutes of imaging each day before and during practice to facilitate greater mastery more quickly. Eventually, you'll build your mental stamina to support imaging during all performance and practice time.

Be sure to include all of the details when you image, particularly deep continuous breathing, and fluid muscular action. Imagine that you are playing with the exact sound, physical sensation and degree of relaxation and ease you ultimately want.

Leg Lifts

Lie on your stomach. Lift your right leg up, keeping it straight and leaving your hip bone on the floor. Lower it slowly. Repeat 10 - 30 times. Then switch to your left leg. Breathe deeply as you do this.

This exercise strengthens the lower back, leg, and stomach muscles.

MOBILITY TESTS

Many of the Muscle Balance Techniques listed in this glossary can be used as tests to determine degree of flexibility or range of motion:

- Hang Over
- Hula Hoops
- Leg Lifts
- Pelvic Tilts
- Pendulum Swings
- Shoulder Rolls

Testing the level of stretch in each muscle group can help you determine how you have been using that area, as well as what activities the muscles now need to balance them. For example, if you use the Hang Over technique and discover that your hands only reach your knees rather than your toes, you now know that you have shortened your leg and lower back muscles excessively and can take action to lengthen those muscles so that you don't develop problems.

See *Stretches* in this section for site-specific stretching exercises.

PELVIC TILTS

Standing: On the exhale, with your knees bent, isolate and rotate your pelvis forward so that your hip bones point toward the ceiling and your buttocks are tucked under.

Then as you inhale, hyper-extend your lower back by pressing the hip bones down toward the floor, lifting your buttocks back and up.

Repeat this movement a number of times slowly and gently while breathing deeply, exhaling as you press forward and inhaling as you hyper-extend.

Sitting: On the exhale, with your legs slightly apart, rotate your pelvis forward so that you are sitting on the "cushioned" area of your buttocks.

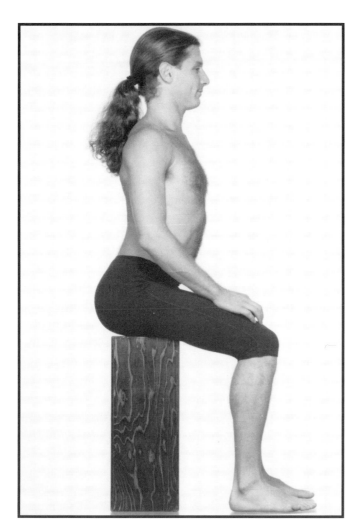

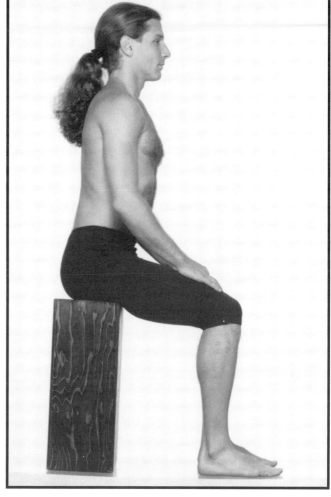

As you inhale, rotate it back till you are on your "sitz" bones and your back is hyper-extended.

These pelvic rotations increase flexibility as well as awareness of the pelvic position. As you play, notice where you tend to place your pelvis and make adjustments so that you find a balanced midpoint.

Pendulum Swings

Stand with your knees slightly bent and your feet aligned under your hips. Turn from side to side, letting your arms swing around until they gently slap you. Do this continuously, using natural momentum to propel you rather than controlled body movement.

This movement massages the lower back, increases flexibility in the spine and pelvis, and teaches the arms to release. This is the kind of release you ultimately want to use while playing.

Pressure Points

A pressure point is a specific spot on the body that is key to relieving stress, tension, or blockage in that region. There are dozens of these points along the meridians of the entire body, and professionals in shiatsu, acupressure, and acupuncture (See DIRECTORY) are trained to heal muscular as well as systemic problems through work on these points.

For our purposes here, we'll focus on points that are particularly helpful for releasing stress in the most chronically tense or overused areas.

Procedure:

Using your thumb or index finger, press into the pressure points indicated on the following diagrams for several minutes each, starting gently and then pressing harder. Breathe deeply and try to relax into the pain or discomfort so that tension isn't referred elsewhere. You can ask a friend to help you by pressing on the points located on your back and shoulders.

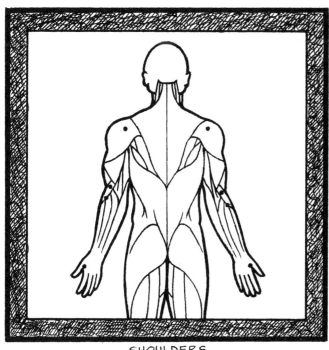

SHOULDERS

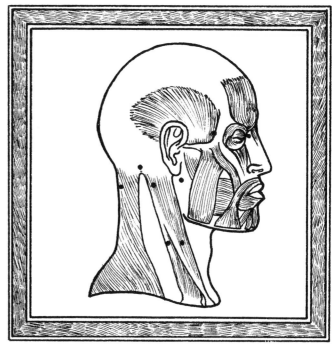

NECK

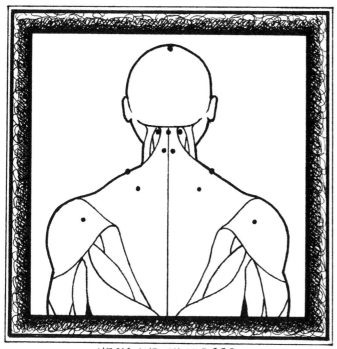

NECK AND SHOULDERS

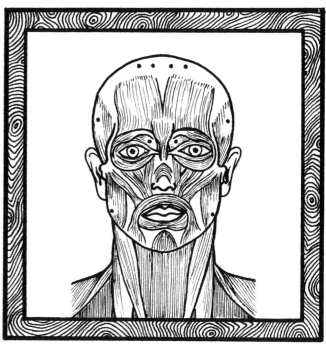

HEAD

Psoas Balancing Technique

The psoas muscle resides in the pelvic bowl, and connects the pelvis to the spine. If one side of the psoas muscle is in spasm, it can pull on the spine and make the shoulder drop on that side, or cause an imbalance in arm or leg length.

Symptoms include lower back, groin, neck, or shoulder pain, and even pain down the inside of the upper leg.

Lie on your back. Extend your arms slowly over your head and maintain a healthy stretch through your fingertips while bringing your palms together.

Keep this hand contact secure and bring your hands into view to check for an imbalance in finger length.

If one hand comes up short, that's the side you need to work on. Place your index finger on the inside of your pelvic bone.

RIB CAGE STRENGTHENER

To give proper support to your arms and shoulders, and to insure torso relaxation and alignment so that the breath can naturally fill your diaphragm, it's important to strengthen and align your torso.

I. Reach your arms straight up and move your upper torso from side to side keeping your hips stationary. This will stretch and lengthen your lower back muscles.

II. With your arms resting on the floor, take a deep breath and expand your rib cage. As you exhale, hold your rib cage open using your intercostal rib muscles. Upon completion of the exhale, release the intercostal muscles and relax. Try this with your arms by your sides as well as with your arms reaching straight up.

You should notice a shift in your spinal alignment as well as an increase in lung capacity. Repeat this several times and use it as a break from practice.

(The *Chest Expansion Stretch* described later in the GLOSSARY can also be used to open and strengthen the upper torso.)

Using your fingertips, press into the area firmly and deeply. You may or may not be able to feel the muscle itself and finger pressure may yield pain and resistance initially, but this will release as you work the area. Breathe deeply. Repeat the test. If you have worked the muscle enough through finger pressure, your hands should meet evenly.

*Note: This technique can help alleviate pain on a short term basis; if the problem persists, see a chiropractor immediately.

Shoulder Rolls

Keeping your arms relaxed, slowly roll both of your shoulders backwards in a circular motion 5 - 10 times. Repeat this movement in a forward direction. Make sure you don't force or crunch your shoulders.

You can also move your shoulders straight forward and then straight back, allowing the chest to cave in and then stretch open in response.

These movements increase flexibility and develop a greater range of motion in the shoulders. This increased flexibility then becomes available to you while playing.

Snaking

Stand with your feet aligned under your hips and your knees bent. Slowly and gently begin to move your torso and your neck in every possible direction — side to side, forward and back — as if you were a snake. Keep your arms and legs passive and fully relaxed. Breathe deeply as you do this. Connect with your sensuality.

Imagine that as you move, someone is pouring warm oil into your spine and joints; allow your movement to be fluid and sensitive, never forced. Stay focused on the activity at hand rather than allowing your mind to wander.

Stomach Strengthener

To support the lower back, it's important to strengthen the lower back's complimentary set of muscles, the stomach muscles. Certain types of sit-ups that are intended to strengthen the stomach actually work the back muscles instead.

To isolate and strengthen the stomach muscles, lie on your back, bend your legs, keeping your feet on the floor, and curl your torso up slightly without pulling from your neck, shoulders, or using your arms to propel you. In this position, pulse about 2 inches up and down at a medium tempo 50 - 100 times. Be sure to keep your elbows out to the sides, not pointing toward the ceiling.

STRETCHES

Stretches help lengthen muscles, thereby balancing any daily activity that would tend to contract them. It's important to stretch slowly and gently while breathing deeply. Don't ever force your muscles to stretch faster or further than they're ready.

You can use the following techniques or make up some of your own:

Yoga Arm Stretches

Place hands behind the back, bringing your palms together. Don't force; if necessary, bring hands partially together lower on the back at first. Hold for 20 - 30 seconds.

This second stretch can be held for 20 - 30 seconds as well. Again, do not force arms into position. If you can't bring the hands together, then only go as far as you can comfortably reach. Then reverse arms so that the right arm reaches over the right shoulder.

Repeat as many times as you like.

Leg Stretches

Breathe deeply as you hold this position for at least 3 - 5 minutes. Use the exhale to gently release over the legs. Never bounce or push.

This stretch will help lengthen the side muscles of the torso as well as the legs. Again, use your breathing to help relax over your leg for 3 - 5 minutes. Don't pull from the shoulder joint.

Repeat each stretch over the opposite leg.

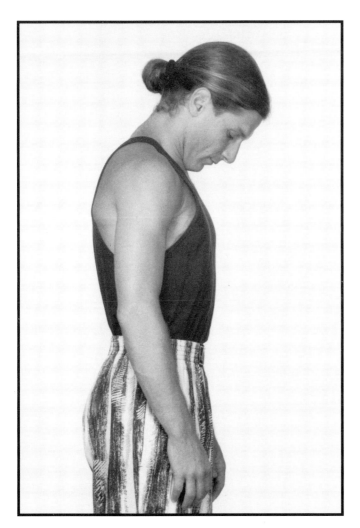 

Neck Stretch

Slowly roll your head forward so that your chin is touching your chest (or as close as you can get it without forcing your head down). Breathe deeply 10 - 15 times. With each breath, gently use the exhale to imagine the muscles in the back of your neck softening and lengthening.

Repeat this with your head rolled back, and then to each side, keeping your torso upright.

Chest Expansion

Lie down on your back and bend your knees, keeping your feet flat on the floor. Now lift your buttocks up off the floor gently, making sure to breathe deeply as you do so. In addition to stretching the chest muscles, this is an excellent stretch for the thigh muscles. Use full, deep breaths to expand the lungs.

TENNIS BALLS

Using two tennis balls, lie on your back, placing one on either side of the spine roughly six inches below the shoulders in the shoulder blade region.

Breathing slowly and deeply, lie on the tennis balls for approximately fifteen minutes. Make sure that you relax completely; you can use the image of releasing your body weight into the floor. As you inhale, keep your body just as relaxed as on the exhale. Then gently remove the balls and lie flat on your back for a few minutes. When you remove the balls, you'll notice that your entire shoulder region is soft to the touch.

Note: Get up slowly afterward. Do not follow with musical or strenuous activity. It's best to work with the balls before a passive activity such as watching television, reading, or going to sleep.

If you are sore the next day, then you did not do this technique correctly. You were probably tensing up while lying on the balls or stiffening up on the inhalation.

The upper back is obviously very difficult to reach with your hands, and the muscles around the shoulder blades and shoulders are used quite strenuously while playing. The tennis balls apply pressure akin to shiatsu or acupressure, signaling the brain to send fresh blood and its own natural painkillers to the area. As clenched muscles relax, lactic acid is released, and this is often uncomfortable. (See *lactic acid* in the unit titled MEDICAL PROBLEMS.)

TRILLS: LIP AND TONGUE

Lip Trills: Keeping the lips close together and relaxed, blow air through them with or without pitch; the sound will resemble a horse's snort!

Tongue Trills: Touch the ridge of the upper palette with the tip of the tongue and blow air through (with or without pitch) allowing the tongue to flutter. You will sound like the "Rrrruffles have rrridges" commercial!

Both trills help to release the tongue and jaw muscles. For instrumentalists who don't require breath to create sound, these trills can keep you breathing as you play: Sing unison pitch using either type of trill while you play a piece of music; if you tend to hold your breath when you play, you will find this exercise difficult at first.

DIRECTORY

Directory

INTRODUCTION

We live in a time when enormous resources are available to us for healing and developmental work. In fact, there are so many resources available that it can be confusing as to which system or approach will be the most useful. Since we are all different composites of mental and physical development and knowledge, we all have different needs.

The *Directory of Physical and Mental Therapies* has been designed to give you an overview of some of the major resources available so that you can make a more informed choice. With the constant emergence of new forms of healing, there is no way that this directory can include all of the systems and tools available; it will, however, give you a good start. Think of the following pages as an inventory of the deluxe supermarket of physical and mental health!

PHYSICAL THERAPIES

Acupressure

Acupuncture

Alexander Technique

Biofeedback

Chiropractic

Feldenkrais

Kinesiology

Massage

Myotherapy

Occupational Therapy

Osteopathy

Physical Therapy

Reflexology

Rolfing

Shiatsu

Touch for Health

Trager

SELF EXERCISE SYSTEMS

Acu-yoga

Aerobics

Dance

Muscle Balance

Tai Chi Chuan

Yoga

Weight Training

MIND AND SPIRIT THERAPIES

Meditation

Structural Consulting

Technologies for Creating

Therapy

HEALING REMEDIES

Ayurveda

Ball Work

Constructive Rest

Herbology

Homeopathy

Hot and Cold

Nutrition

Physical Therapies

ACUPRESSURE

Acupressure promotes circulation, freedom of movement in the joints and muscles and release of muscular tension through prolonged and gentle finger pressure into key acupuncture points along the body's meridians. It was developed many centuries ago in China and has been used quite effectively to dissolve tension and blockage from all parts of the body, encouraging energy and blood to flow more easily, thereby helping the body to heal its own problems, especially problems caused by tension and stress.

ACUPUNCTURE

Acupuncture, an ancient Oriental health practice, utilizes slender needles, inserted at various points along the energy meridians that course through the body, to balance and normalize the energy flow and restore health. Needles can be used to anesthetize areas of the body or cure numerous health afflictions, including arthritis and muscular maladies.

ALEXANDER TECHNIQUE

Developed by actor Matthias Alexander in the late 1800's to heal his dysfunctional voice, the Alexander technique addresses unconscious bad habits in relationship to posture and the way the body is used, and trains the student to release tension. It is a process of re-educating individuals to move with a minimum of muscular effort.

Using hand contact, the Alexander teacher gently informs the student's body of new postural possibilities. Students are encouraged to take at least thirty lessons to help break habitual (and energy inefficient) patterns that have developed around simple activities such as standing up, sitting down, and walking. The work makes a strong contribution toward ease of musical performance, and the new body alignment frees the breath.

BIOFEEDBACK

Biofeedback was developed in the early 1970's. It utilizes an instrument that monitors physiological response to mental processes with electrodes or transducers. Since our nervous system tends to link certain activities with certain levels of tension, even thinking about playing one's musical instrument or talking about playing is sufficient to trigger muscle memory. The client, by watching the meter and thinking or talking about playing his or her instrument, can see and then learn to control functions such as muscle tension, blood pressure, and heart rate.

CHIROPRACTIC

Developed by Daniel David Palmer in 1895, modern chiropractics uses manual manipulation of the spine to promote overall physical health. Because the vertebrae contain and protect the spinal cord, through which nerve impulses flow, manual adjustment is used to correct misaligned spinal segments that would otherwise impinge on nerve impulses.

Chiropractic doctors use varying techniques to accomplish this; some are gentle, using non-force, others are more aggressive. In addition, some chiropractors use a cranial adjustment, centering the cranium through gentle pressure on the roof of the mouth.

Chiropractors who are trained to use Touch for Health, an outgrowth of Kinesiology, can tailor your adjustment on a visit-by-visit basis by using simple muscle tests to determine weaknesses in the system.

FELDENKRAIS

Moshe Feldenkrais developed a series of ingenious and powerful exercises for the reorganization of the body. These simple movements increase sensitivity, improve posture, and heighten personal awareness. Since how we live in and use our bodies is so deeply molded by childhood education and experience, the opportunity to re-educate our bodies on a very basic level opens the way to mental and physical integration and the development of a new, invigorated whole self.

KINESIOLOGY

Kinesiology is a diagnostic and therapeutic technique that pinpoints areas of physical and emotional dysfunction by measuring muscle strength. Weak muscles often indicate health problems in corresponding organs or related areas of the body. By stimulating specific points along the body's meridians, it is possible to strengthen weak muscles or relax muscles in spasm, thereby positively effecting the corresponding area. The technique incorporates the principles of acupressure in order to promote an even flow of energy throughout the body.

MASSAGE

There are a number of approaches to massage but in general massage is a gentle, hands-on way of promoting both total body circulation and the release of the tension and toxins accumulated from daily wear and tear. Additionally, massage facilitates muscle relaxation. Whether you massage yourself or go to a professional, massage is a wonderful way of nurturing yourself; it is so pleasurable, that you are basically giving yourself a gentle, loving message that you are important.

MYOTHERAPY

Myotherapy is a form of muscle therapy originated by Dr. Desmond Tivy and Bonnie Pruden in 1976. Muscle pain is relieved through applying pressure to trigger points: tight or tender spots in the muscles.

OCCUPATIONAL THERAPY

The occupational therapist deals primarily with the upper extremities — the head, neck, and trunk. The therapy is focused on the rehabilitation of patients with neurological disorders (such as cerebral palsy) or accident victims. Prescribed creative physical activity carried out under supervision is used to promote recovery or rehabilitation following disease or injury. Devices such as splinting (used to keep a disease-disabled muscle from contracting) and contraptions that aid disabled limbs are also used to help the patient cope with daily routine functions.

OSTEOPATHY

Built on sixteen years of careful study by Dr. Andrew Taylor Still in the late 1800's, osteopathy is one of many forms of healing by manipulation (which has been used in one way or another since Hippocrates' time). Osteopathy concerns itself with the neuro-muscular-skeletal system, or more specifically, the dynamic interplay between nerves, muscles, surrounding fibrous tissue, and bones. Manipulation is designed to reduce muscular tension, improve joint motion, and relieve pressure or congestion around nerve roots. Sometimes surgery, drugs, or ultra-sound are used as adjuncts.

PHYSICAL THERAPY

The physical therapist uses manual medicine (hands-on manipulation) in combination with heat, ice, ultra-sound and electrical stimulation. Physical therapy focuses on musculo-skeletal problems and clients tend to include athletes, dancers, musicians, and people in occupations that cause repetitive strain injury. The essence of the therapy is to promote fluid (blood) flow. Because injured areas often swell, blood flow is restricted. When blood is able to flow more freely again, nutrients and oxygen can be transported to the site of injury, and toxins and detritus can be transported out. The area is then better able to heal itself.

REFLEXOLOGY

Reflexology is a form of therapeutic foot and hand massage. All of the body's nerves have endings in the feet and hands. When there is an imbalance or weakness in any area of the body, it is reflected in the corresponding point in the hands and feet, and crystallized calcium and acid deposits accumulate over the nerve endings where these points are located. By pressing on these points the crystals can be broken up and dissolved; at the same time, the nerves are stimulated to help heal the related area of the body.

ROLFING

Rolfing is a method of deep tissue massage that focuses on manipulating the body into a correct postural position. It was developed in the 1930's by Ida Rolf and gained popularity during the sixties. Rolfing acknowledges that the body's shape has been chiefly affected by emotional and psychological ways of relating to the world. The actual rolfing process involves loosening and lengthening specific muscles and fascia (the connective tissue that houses muscles, tendons, lymph nodes, ligaments, etc.), enabling the patient to release tensions arising from internal conflicts and childhood defenses, thereby freeing the body's energies.

SHIATSU

Shiatsu uses firm, rhythmic pressure along acupuncture meridians. This eliminates fatigue and promotes stamina and vitality. While shiatsu can ease pain, tension, and chronic problems, its emphasis is on prevention of illness through stimulation of the body's natural curative powers. Shiatsu is similar to acupressure, though the practitioner's finger pressure techniques can differ.

TOUCH FOR HEALTH

Touch for Health was designed by chiropractor Dr. George Goodheart, who developed the field of Kinesiology to determine the state of energy and health in each of the body's systems. Through research he was able to identify the relationship between specific muscle groups, corresponding organs and their acupuncture meridians. He then developed a series of simple muscle tests for diagnosing and relieving imbalances in the body's energy systems. Many chiropractors include Touch for Health as a regular preliminary to treatment.

TRAGER

Trager work is a unique non-intrusive approach to body work and movement re-education. It uses gentle and rhythmic movements to facilitate the release of holding patterns in the body-mind and to restore free-flowing movement and self-expression. It was created by Milton Trager.

Self Exercise Systems

ACU-YOGA

Acu-yoga was developed by Michael Reed Gach, author, healer, and director of the Acupressure Institute in Berkeley, California. It combines the gentle stretches and postures of yoga, which originated in India, and the healing points of acupressure, which came from China, to provide a balanced system of healing and rejuvenation for the relief of stress, stiffness, and muscle strain.

AEROBICS

Aerobic activity includes any activity that increases heart rate and breathing through sustained, continuous movement, including jogging, bicycling, or using a rowing machine, for example. Aerobics classes are movement classes designed to achieve this end through a continuous and fast-paced series of exercises. A good class should start with some slow warm-up stretches and work into quicker movements that increase the heart rate and raise the body temperature. "Low impact" aerobics classes tend to be gentler on the body while "high impact" classes are apt to cause more wear and tear on the ankle, knee, and hip joints.

DANCE

Modern, jazz, and ballet dance classes provide the body with stretching and aerobic activity. Muscles have an opportunity to be worked out and strengthened in a variety of ways, helping to counteract the focused and repetitious activity of playing an instrument. Ballet tends to be a more rigid series of body moves, which isn't helpful to developing a more fluid and relaxed style of using the body. Musicians are therefore recommended to take classes in modern or jazz dance.

MUSCLE BALANCE

The name and concept was developed by Julie Lyonn Lieberman but the actual physical movements can come from any and all physical disciplines. Muscle Balance is the daily practice of utilizing a system of physical exercises to strengthen and balance muscle groups that are ordinarily used in a limited and repetitive fashion, whether from playing a musical instrument, or performing a particular job or task. The movements should counteract repetitive use as well as build a support system, so that isolated muscles need not bear the brunt of repetitive activities.

TAI CHI CHUAN

While tai chi is actually a martial art form, many of its practitioners use it for the healthful purposes of developing strength, vitality, and mental focus. Dating back to first century China, the tai chi "form," as it is called, consists of a series of linked movements and positions that almost look like a slow-motion dance. Tai means "great" or "original"; Chi means "life force or energy"; chuan means "fist" or "boxing."

YOGA

Yoga is a 6000 year-old philosophy and practice that embraces health of mind, body, and spirit. There are four main types of Yoga: *Gnana* (spiritual), *Bhakti* (emotional), *Raja* (mental), and *Hatha* (physical). Hatha Yoga is most well known in the West and consists of three main practices: the *kriyas* (cleansings), *asanas* (postures), and *pranayama* (breath control).

Some of the results obtained from practicing Hatha Yoga include increased agility and alignment of the spine, a revitalization of the endocrine system and the internal organs, and a heightened control over the nervous system, enabling the individual to achieve a state of deep relaxation.

WEIGHT TRAINING

Health clubs have popularized weight training with the Universal and Nautilus machines. Muscular development using weight resistance can strengthen all of the muscle groups so that there is greater support available for focused physical activity.

Lighter weights with more repetitions are recommended for musicians rather than heavier weights; the muscles are less likely to knot up or be overworked. Be sure to breathe deeply during weight training, and balance with stretches and aerobic activity. Allow at least one day off between workouts to give your body a chance to rest.

Mind and Spirit Therapies

While there are numerous therapeutic systems in this category, and every year brings the development of more, only a few are mentioned here. These were selected to represent substantially different schools of thought.

MEDITATION

A meditation session can take place alone or in a group. There are a variety of different meditation disciplines but the approach is basically the same; slow, deep breathing is used as the individual practices focusing his or her mind for a given period of time on a daily basis. Normal daydreaming and the wandering of the mind are reduced and sometimes even eliminated as the mind remains focused, (on a sound, a repeated phrase, or image), creating a sense of calm and inner peace. Meditation lowers blood pressure, facilitates muscular relaxation, improves health, and increases an individual's ability to concentrate.

STRUCTURAL CONSULTING

Structural Consulting, created by Robert Fritz, consists of one two to three-hour session between consultant and client. During this time the consultant asks questions designed to reveal the underlying structure of the stated problem. The consultant builds a picture of the information presented by the client without interpretation or an attempt to force-fit the information into a preconceived theory. This technique enables the consultant to see the underlying structure more clearly. As the session proceeds, unconscious behavioral strategies give way to reveal the actual structures and underlying beliefs at play.

TECHNOLOGIES FOR CREATING

The Technologies for Creating Basic course is a five-week course designed to teach you how to be more effective as a creator. Approaching creativity as an innate skill that can be developed, the course offers simple and powerful methods that can help you consistently produce the results you want in your life. The Basic course will help you to understand the principles and structure of how to create. In addition, some of the techniques offered help increase focus, awareness, and health. Follow-up courses are available as well as weekend workshops.

THERAPY

There are numerous systems of therapy. A therapy session is generally held between the client and the therapist, although there are group therapy sessions available. While therapy was originally developed to treat mental illness, many therapeutic systems now focus on helping the healthy-minded individual be more effective in his or her life. The styles of work range from psychoanalysis, which is introspective and long-term therapy, to "acting out" problems, developing creative behavioral alternatives in stress-related situations, and so on. The emphasis is generally on learning how to see and verbalize the truth about one's feelings and interactions, and establishing more effective, satisfying behavior and communication styles.

Healing Remedies

AYURVEDA

Ayurveda is a 3,000 year-old healing tradition originated in India. Ayurveda describes three doshas, each representing a fundamental controlling principle in human physiology. *Vata* pertains to movement, the nervous system, and elimination; *pitta* relates to heat, metabolism, and digestion; and *kapha* involves structural aspects of the physiology responsible for biological strength and resistance. Our inner ecology is determined by the predominance of one constitutional, or doshic, factor. The patient's imbalance holds the secret of the treatment, and the healing process generally includes internal purification techniques, herbalized steam and oil treatments, neuromuscular/neurorespiratory integration, colonics, purgations, meditation, dietary adjustment, and massage.

BALL WORK

Dancer and choreographer Elaine Summers developed a whole series of exercises using hollow rubber balls to help the muscles release tension and achieve increased pliability. The balls are placed under various parts of the body singly, in pairs, or as many as five — which completely lifts the student off the ground. This frees the spine from its usual relationship to gravity. By placing the body in a position for which there is no muscle memory, the balls help to overcome habitual posture. Acting as a flotation device, suspending the body in space, the balls facilitate multidirectional movement and allow exploration of positions that would otherwise be difficult to achieve. They provide a focal point — a psychic device to increase concentration and meditation. Supervision is recommended when first using balls. (See *Tennis Balls* in GLOSSARY.)

CONSTRUCTIVE REST

See *Constructive Rest* in GLOSSARY.

HERBOLOGY

Herbologists test the pulse to determine the health of each of the four major systems in the body: respiratory, circulatory, endocrine, and digestive. They combine this information with the client's specific complaints and medical history. A daily herbal combination is then designed to aid the body in healing itself. While drugs are synthesized chemicals and as such often have degenerative side effects, herbs are of natural composition. They are actual foods and have powerful healing ability with little or no negative effect.

HOMEOPATHY

Homeopathy is based on the principle that "like cures like" and was developed by the German physician Dr. Samuel Hahnemann in the early 1800's. (Traditional western medicine is aleopathic, or based on the principle that "unlike" cures like.) Homeopathic remedies consist largely of herbs, and often the cure is the same as the malady. In curing an allergic reaction to a hornet's bite, let's say, a homeopathist would be likely to give you a diluted extract of hornet or bee venom (like) rather than an antihistamine (unlike). The body's natural healing powers are honored and stimulated and the individual is viewed wholistically: life style, nutrition, and emotional and psychological factors are all taken into account while determining the best course of treatment.

HOT AND COLD

See GLOSSARY.

NUTRITION

This is obviously too large a field to discuss in any detail here. But there are certain basic guidelines to follow if you are healing a muscular condition or improving your general tone and energy.

Certain foods are particularly helpful to the overall health of the muscles. They contain nutrients such as calcium, the B vitamin family, vitamin C, and protein. Other foods are thought to be irritating or degenerative to muscle tissue. It's important to be aware of which foods have a positive effect on your energy, stamina and health, and which foods tend to make you feel jittery, tired or irritable.

Go to your local health food store and research foods that are especially valuable in building health, particularly foods that contain nutrients such as calcium, the B family, vitamin C and protein. You might also want to learn about different healthful diet regimens such as macrobiotics or food combining.

YOU ARE YOUR INSTRUMENT

APPENDIX

Suggested References

Benjamin, Dr. Ben. *Listen to Your Pain*. New York: Penguin Books, 1984.

Bertherat, Therese, and Bernstein, Carol. *The Body Has Its Reasons*. New York: Avon Books, 1979.

Bevan, Dr. James. *Anatomy and Physiology*. New York: Simon and Schuster, 1978.

Blakeslee, Thomas. *The Right Brain*. New York: Doubleday and Company, Inc., 1980.

Brodnitz, Friedrich. *Keep Your Voice Healthy*. Boston: Little, Brown and Company, Inc., 1973.

Brown, Barbara. *Stress and the Art of Biofeedback*. New York: Bantam Books, 1977.

Bry, Adelaide. *Visualization: Directing the Movies of Your Mind*. New York: Barnes & Noble Books, 1976.

Buzan, Tony. *Use Both Sides of Your Brain*. New York: E.P. Dutton, 1983.

Chopra, Dr. Deepak. *Quantum Healing*. New York: Bantam, 1990.

Chopra, Dr. Deepak. *Return of the Rishi*. Boston: Houghton Mifflin Co., 1988.

Connelly, Dianne. *Traditional Acupuncture: The Law of the Five Elements*. Maryland: The Center for Traditional Acupuncture, 1975.

Deva, Jeannie. *The Contemporary Vocalist*. Cambridge: The Voice Studio, 1991. (To order, write: Rock Publications, P.O. Box 374, Astor Station, Boston, MA 02123-0374)

Diamond, John. *The Life Energy in Music*, Volumes I, II and III. New York: Archaeus Press, 1981.

Feldenkrais, Moshe. *Awareness Through Movement*. New York: Harper and Row, 1972.

Fry, Hunter J.H. "Overuse Syndrome in Musicians — 100 Years Ago." *The Medical Journal of Australia*, December, 1986.

Fry, Hunter J.H. "What's in a Name?" *Medical Problems of Performing Artists*, March, 1986.

Gach, Michael Reed. *Acu-Yoga*. New York: Japan Publications, 1981.

Gach, Michael Reed. *The Bum Back Book*. Berkeley: Acu Press, 1983.

Gach, Michael Reed. *Greater Energy at Your Fingertips*. Berkeley: Celestial Arts, 1986.

Graffman, Gary. "Doctor, Can You Lend an Ear?" *Medical Problems of Performing Artists*; March 1986.

Havas, Kato. *Stage Fright*. London: Bosworth, 1973.

Houston, Jean. *The Possible Human*. Los Angeles: J.P. Tarcher, Inc., 1982.

Lederman, Dr. Richard, and Calabrese, Leonard. "Overuse Syndrome in Instrumentalists." *Medical Problems of Performing Artists*, March, 1986.

Lockwood, Dr. Alan. "Medical Problems of Musicians." *The New England Journal of Medicine*, Volume 320, No. 4, January 26, 1989.

Loehr, Dr. James, and Migdow, Dr. Jeffrey. *Take A Deep Breath*. New York: Villard Books, A Division of Random House, 1986.

Nies, Dr. Alan. "Clinical Pharmacology of Beta-Adrenergic Blockers." *Medical Problems of Performing Artists*, March 1986.

Ohashi, Waturu. *Do-it-Yourself SHIATSU*. Toronto: Clarke, Irwin & Co., 1976.

Springer, Sally, and Deutsch, Georg. *Left Brain, Right Brain*. New York: Freman and Company, 1981.

Ward, Milton. *The Brilliant Function of Pain*. New York: Optimus Books, 1977.

Resource Organizations

Acupressure:
Acupressure Institute
1533 Shattuck Ave
Berkleley, CA 94709   (415-845-1059)

Acupuncture:
American Association of Acupuncture & Oriental Medicine
1424 16th Street NW, Suite 501
Washington DC 20036   (202-265-2287)

Alexander Technique:
The N. A. Society of Teachers of the Alexander Technique
PO Box 3992
Champaign, IL 61826   (217-359-3529)

Ayurvedic Medicine:
Maharishi Ayurveda Association of America
PO Box 282
Fairfield, IA 52556   (515-472-8477)

Chiropractic:
American Chiropractic Association
1701 Clarendon Blvd.
Arlington, VA 22209   (703-276-8800)

Feldenkrais:
The Feldenkrais Guild
PO Box 11145
San Franciscos, CA 94101   (415-550-8708)

Foot Reflexology:
The International Institute of Reflexology
PO Box 12642
St. Petersburg, FL 33733   (813-343-4811)

Herbology:
American Herb Association
PO Box 99
Rescue, CA 95672

Holistic Medicine:
American Holistic Medical Association
4101 Lake Boone Trail, Suite 201
Raleigh, NC 27607   (919-787-5146)

Homeopathy:
National Center for Homeopathy
1500 Massachusettes Ave NW, Suite 42
Washington DC 20005   (202-223-6182)

Massage Therapy:
American Massage Therapy Association
1130 W. North Shore Ave
Chicago, IL 60626   (312-761-2682)

Music Improvisation:
Music for People
Rd 4, Box 221A
Keene, NH 03431   (603-352-4941)

Music Instruction on cassette and video:
Homespun Tapes
Box 694
Woodstock NY 12498   (914-679-7832)
                                     (800-338-2737)

Technologies for Creating:
Box 116
Williamsville, VT 05362   (800-722-1661)

Trager:
The Trager Instittute
10 Old Mill St
Mill Valley, CA 94941   (415-388-2688)

Rolfing:
Rolf Instittute
PO Box 1868
Boulder Co 80306   (303-449-5903)

Index

V

verbal approach   20, 28, 80
verbal instruction   79
video order form 146
visual   93
visual memory   23
visualization   23, 26
visualization techniques   71
visualize   16

W

warm-up process   84
waterbugs   34
Weight Training   134
weightlessness   35
whole-brain thinking   80
will-power   16

Y

yoga   14, 134
Yoga Arm Stretches 123

Video Order Form

The *You Are Your Instrument Video* is a companion piece to the book. While enhancing the material from the book, it has been designed to function as a separate resource.

Now you can see and hear *You Are Your Instrument*! Join Julie Lyonn Lieberman in an informal studio setting as she personally:

- explains many new approaches to music-making

- leads you in a number of powerfully useful mental and physical techniques

- uses live musicians to illustrate important concepts that are key to fluid, pain-free music-making

- interacts with a professional physical fitness model to demonstrate all of the muscle balance techniques outlined in her book

YOU ARE YOUR INSTRUMENT FOR INSTRUMENTALISTS:

This exciting two-hour video will lead you through a number of mental and physical exercises designed to help you improve your practice habits, and teach you how to use the muscles and joints in harmony with anatomy.

Also included are individual segments in which Julie presents detailed information on the specific challenges of the bowed, fretted, wind and keyboard/percussion instrument families. Through interaction with experienced musicians in each of these fields, Julie will demonstrate many new mental and physical approaches to practice and performance.

YOU ARE YOUR INSTRUMENT FOR VOCALISTS:

On this unique two-hour video, Julie explores such important issues for vocalists as singing from whole brain/whole body, breath support and control, vocal stamina, the causes of vocal dysfunction and injury, and the effect of diet and environment on the body's ability to produce sound well.

She is joined by three experts in the field: Maitland Peters, professor of voice at Manhattan School of Music, Jeannie Deva, author of *The Contemporary Vocalist*, and Katie Agresta, teacher to such artists as Phoebe Snow, Cyndi Lauper and Bon Jovi.

To Order:

Call 1-800-338-2737 or write to Homespun Tapes, P.O. Box 694, Woodstock, N.Y. 12498
Price: $49.95. Visa or Mastercard accepted. (Add 7% sales tax if delivery is in New York State)
Postage and Handling: U.S. and Cananda $4.00, Europe and South America: $12.00,
Africa, Asia and Australia: $20.00

Book Order Form

Please send _____ copies of *You Are Your Instrument* to:

_____
Name

_____
Address

_____
City   State   Zip

Price
$19.95, U.S. Currency

Sales tax:
New York State residents add 7% sales tax.
New York City residents add 8 $1/4$% sales tax.

Shipping:
Book Rate: $2.00 for the first book and .75 for each additional book.
(Surface shipping may take three to four weeks)
Air Mail: $3 per book.
Canada and foreign, $3.50 for the first book and 1.00 for each additional book.

Payment:
Make check payable to:
Huiksi Music
P.O. Box 495
New York, N.Y. 10024

For information about Julie Lyonn Lieberman's other books, *Blues Fiddle* and *Improvising Violin*, or *The Talking Violin*, her National Public Radio Series now available as a cassette series, write to: Huiksi Music, P.O. Box 495, New York, NY 10024 or leave your name and address on the electronic mail machine: 212-713-5515.

You Are Your Instrument is

"…an important addition to the growing field of Performance Medicine. The exercises and practice suggestions are carefully thought out and a great asset to musical injury prevention."

DR. RICHARD NORRIS, M.D.

"…solidly researched, very well organized, clearly written and illustrated, and if not encyclopedic at least impressively broad in scope."

TED RUST, MUSIC FOR THE LOVE OF IT

"…a novel, helpful manual of interest to any musician."

THE SMALL PRESS BOOK REVIEW

"…a must for every musician's library. I am excited about learning to play in a fluid, pain-free way. The insights from your book are sure to be very helpful in the weeks (and years!) to come. Already I can feel a difference every time I sit down with the instrument."

BILL OCHS, PENNYWHISTLER'S PRESS

"…both a practice and performance guide and a key to playing in a fluid, pain-free manner."

THE BOOKWATCH

"There I was at practice last night. And then, before I played I took a moment to check out my body and its relationship to the violin and bow. That's when it hit me, and I wanted to smile. Was I embracing these treasured pieces as I would a close friend? Yes…I could feel my heart and soul say 'come closer…I want to hold on to you, you mean so much to me.' I was holding on, without the usual tension, and suddenly I could play as fast as my mind could hear. This was a revelation, because my usual mode of living is to simultaneously push away from me (distance myself from) those I love, while longing to embrace them. Thank you Julie."

MYRA FRANKS, VIOLINIST

About the Author

Julie Lyonn Lieberman is an improvising violinist, singer, producer, composer, educator, and recording artist. The author of *Blues Fiddle, Improvising Violin,* and *The Hobo Violin,* Julie has three recordings of original music, *Empathic Connections, Arcturus,* and *The Roaring Brook Fiddler* to her credit. She teaches privately in New York City and has led workshops throughout the East Coast for the past fifteen years at such colleges as Manhattan School of Music, William Paterson College, Berklee School of Music, Hunter College, and New England Conservatory, among others. Her National Public Radio series, *The Talking Violin,* premiered in 1989, and is now available as a cassette series. In addition, her instructional tape series, *Improvising Violin,* as well as *You Are Your Instrument* on video, is available through Homespun Tapes. She can be reached through Huiksi Music.